Dyslexia friendly

CW01597053

Exam Mastery Series

GCSE and International GCSE

# Foundation Maths A

250 Challenging
Exam Style Questions

Olivia Press

# Introduction

Do you still need more work on the last few tough questions that come up in papers?

Are you confident in answering questions that tell you exactly what to do but find multi-step and worded questions challenging?

Do you want to strengthen your problem-solving skills before the real exam?

If you answered yes to any of these, then this book is for you.

# What is included

- 250 multi-step and problem solving exam-style questions
- Questions written in a similar format to those found in real GCSE and International GCSE Maths papers
- Answers at the end of the book
- Full worked solutions available online at: **www.oliviapresspublishers.com**

# What you will need

- A notebook
- Usual maths stationery
- Scrap paper (for rough workings and notes)
- Scientific Calculator
- GCSE students can use a calculator unless they see this symbol 
- International GCSE students can use a calculator for all questions as their IGCSE exams are calculator exams.

# How to use this book

- Follow the study plan inside (10 questions per set) or create a timetable that works best for you — and stick to it.
- Try not to use a calculator where possible to sharpen your calculation skills.
- Don't be afraid to feel stuck. Avoid checking the answers too quickly — remember, in the real exam you won't have them.
- Allow time for reflection after each set. Make notes about what you found difficult. Knowing what you need to work on is a crucial step in achieving your goals.
- If you are making mistakes, that's a positive sign — it means you are learning and improving.
- Finally, be proud of your own achievements! It does not matter how slow you go – you are progressing and learning!

**Exam Mastery Series**

GCSE and International GCSE

# Foundation Maths A

250 Challenging Exam Style Questions

## Contents



**Foundation Maths B**

*For every student who keeps trying,*
*even when the question*
*feels impossible.*

# Chapter 1
# Algebra

*"You don't learn to walk by following rules. You learn by doing, and by falling over." – Richard Branson*

Worked Solutions

# Algebra: Worked examples

**Here are three worked examples to get you started on this topic.**

- **Look at each example in turn.**
- **Can you do the question independently?**
- **If not, go over it slowly and work through the solution.**

### Worked example 1

Apples are sold in small packs of 4 and large bags of 7.
Roxy buys $x$ small packs of apples and $y$ large bags of apples.
She buys a total of $T$ apples.
Write a formula for $T$ in terms of $x$ and $y$. **(3 marks)**

### Solution

| | |
|---|---|
| One small pack has 4 apples.<br>Two small packs have 2 × 4 = 8 apples<br>Three small packs have 3 × 4 = 12 apples<br>$x$ small packs have $x \times 4 = 4x$ apples **(1 mark)** | When multiplying a letter by a number, you just place them next to each other – number first, then the letter.<br>For example,<br>$x \times 4$ or $4 \times x = 4x$ |
| One large bag has 7 apples.<br>Two large bags have 2 × 7 = 14 apples<br>Three large bags have 3 × 7 = 21 apples<br>$y$ large bags have $y \times 7 = 7y$ apples **(1 mark)** | |
| Total = $4x + 7y$ **(1 mark)** | Watch out!<br>$4x + 7y$ is not $11xy$.<br>You cannot combine terms in $x$ with terms in $y$ when you add or subtract. |

## Worked example 2

The area of rectangle A is equal to the area of rectangle B.
All measurements are in centimetres.

**a)** Show that $12x - 24 = 8x$ **(2 marks)**

**b)** Find $x$. **(2 marks)**

**c)** Work out the perimeter of rectangle B. **(2 marks)**

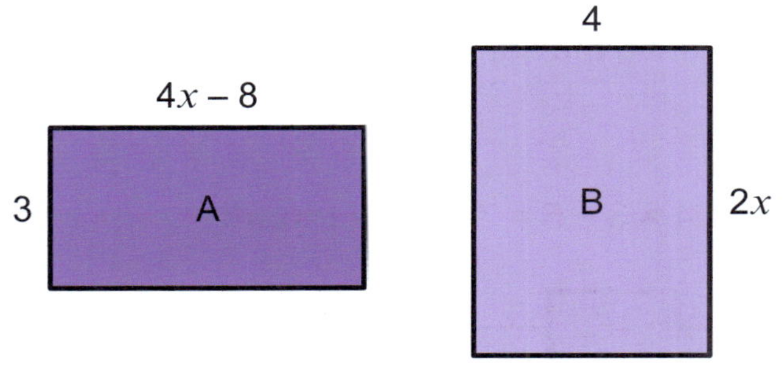


not drawn accurately

## Solution

| | |
|---|---|
| **a)** area of A = $3(4x - 8)$<br>area of B = $4 \times 2x$ **(1 mark)**<br>area of A = area of B<br>$3(4x - 8) = 4 \times 2x$<br>$12x - 24 = 8x$ **(1 mark)** | Find area of rectangle A.<br>Find area of rectangle B.<br>Make them equal to each other. |
| **b)** $12x - 24 = 8x$ ↓Now add 24 to both sides<br>$12x = 8x + 24$ ↓Now subtract $8x$ from both sides **(1 mark)**<br>$4x = 24$ ↓Now divide both sides by 4<br>$x = 6$ **(1 mark)** | Solve the equation you formed in part **a)**. |
| **c)** $2x = 2 \times 6 = 12$<br>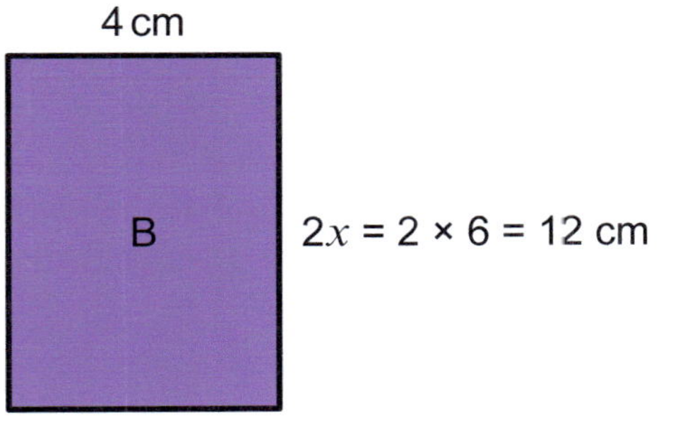<br>perimeter of B = 4 cm + 12 cm + 4 cm + 12 cm **(1 mark)**<br>= 32 cm **(1 mark)** | Remember there are four sides of the rectangle. |

## Worked example 3

Here is a number machine.

input → ×3 → −5 → output

**a)** Work out the **output** when the input is 4 **(1 mark)**

**b)** Work out the **input** when the output is 13 **(2 marks)**

**c)** Show that there is a value of the input for which the input and the output have the same value. **(3 marks)**

### Solution

**a)** When input = 4, output = 4 × 3 − 5 = 7 **(1 mark)**

**b)** input → ×3 → −5 → output = 13

input = 6 ← 18 ÷ 3 = 6 ← 13 + 5 = 18

13 + 5 = 18 **(1 mark)**

18 ÷ 3 = 6 **(1 mark)**

Input = 6

Start from the right-hand side.

output = 13

Now travel from right to left through the number machine, reversing each operation.

**c)** Suppose there is a number $x$ for which input = $x$ and output = $x$

$x \times 3 - 5 = x$ **(1 mark)**

$3x - 5 = x$ ↓Now add 5 to both sides

$3x = x + 5$ ↓Now subtract $x$ from both sides **(1 mark)**

$2x = 5$ ↓Now divide both sides by 2

$x = 2.5$ **(1 mark)**

Form and solve an equation using $x$ as the input and the output.

Now try each set of questions.

You might want to create a table like this in your exercise book to record your progress.

You could try and complete the 10 questions in each set, in a single study session.

This may help with exam practice and keeping the focus going even when the questions are challenging.

| Study session | Question set | Tick when completed | How do I feel about these questions? Difficult – I need to improve my understanding of … |
|---|---|---|---|
| 1 | A | | |
| 2 | B | | |
| 3 | C | | |
| 4 | D | | |
| 5 | E | | |

Remember, there is no 'quick fix' when problem solving. If you are stuck, this is a good thing. It means you are being challenged and you are learning.

Worked Solutions are here **https://www.oliviapresspublishers.com**

**All diagrams** in this chapter are not drawn accurately unless otherwise stated.

**GCSE students** can use a calculator unless they see this symbol 

**International GCSE students** can use a calculator in all the questions.

## Algebra Set A

**A1.** Pens are sold in small and large packets.
There are 6 pens in a small packet.
There are 15 pens in a large packet.
Jake buys $d$ small packets and $f$ large packets.
He buys a total of $T$ pens.
Write a formula for $T$ in terms of $d$ and $f$. **(3 marks)**

**A2.** Said is $n$ years old.
Isla is twice as old as Said.
Leo is five years older than Said.
The sum of Said's age, Isla's age and Leo's age is $T$ years.
Find and simplify a formula for $T$ in terms of $n$. **(3 marks)**

**A3.** There are $x$ rows of seats in the school theatre.
There are 20 seats in each row.

**a)** Write an expression, in terms of $x$, for the total number of seats in the theatre. **(1 mark)**

The theatre is almost full. There are only 5 empty spaces.

**b)** Write an expression, in terms of $x$, for the total number of people in the theatre. **(1 mark)**

There are 255 people in the theatre.

**c)** How many rows of seats are there in the school theatre? **(2 marks)**

**A4.** Here are four straight rods.

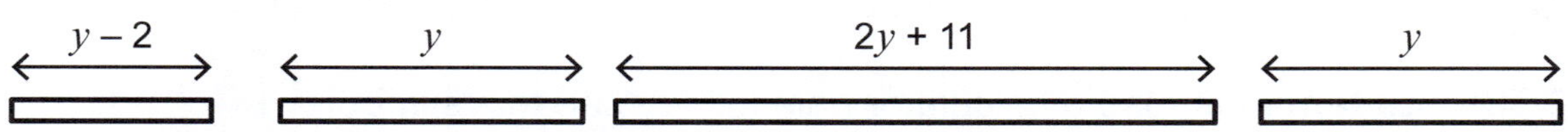


All measurements are in centimetres.
The total length of the four rods is $T$ cm.

**a)** Find a formula for $T$ in terms of $y$.
Write your formula as simply as possible. **(2 marks)**

**b)** The total length of the four rods is 64 cm.
Find the length of the shortest rod. **(3 marks)**

**A5.** Batteries are sold in packets and in boxes.
There are 4 batteries in a packet.
There are 20 batteries in a box.
Sameena buys one box of batteries. She takes $t$ batteries out of the box.

**a)** Write down an expression, in terms of $t$, for the number of batteries left in the box. **(1 mark)**

**b)** Kourtney buys $x$ packets of batteries and $y$ boxes of batteries.
Write down an expression, in terms of $x$ and $y$, for the total number of batteries Kourtney buys. **(3 marks)**

**A6.** Beth has a biased coin.
When she tosses the coin once, the probability of getting tails is $x$.

**a)** Write down an expression, in terms of $x$, for the probability of getting heads. **(1 mark)**

> Probabilities always add up to 1.

Beth tosses the coin 150 times.

**b)** Write down an expression, in terms of $x$, to estimate the number of times the coin lands on heads.
Simplify your answer. **(2 marks)**

**A7.** The area of rectangle A is equal to the area of rectangle B.

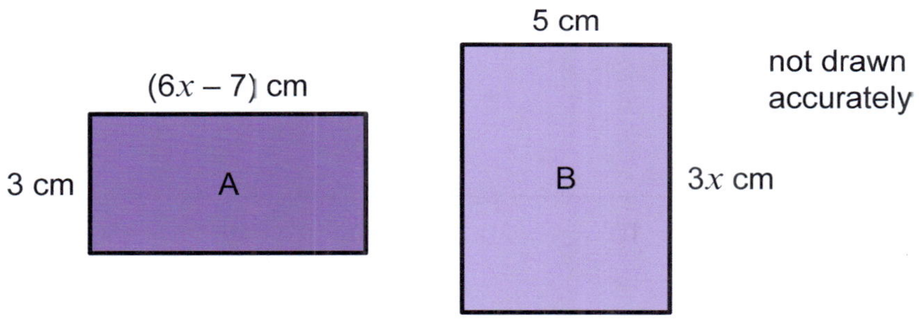


**a)** Show that $18x - 21 = 15x$. **(2 marks)**

**b)** Find $x$. **(2 marks)**

**c)** Work out the perimeter of rectangle B. **(2 marks)**

**A8.** Here is a number machine.

input → ×2 → –8 → output

**a)** Work out the **output** when the input is 5 **(2 marks)**

**b)** Work out the **input** when the output is 5 **(2 marks)**

**c)** If you input the number $x$, the output will also be $x$.
Find the value of $x$. **(3 marks)**

**A9.** Max uses his car to deliver parcels.
You can use this graph to find the delivery cost for different distances.

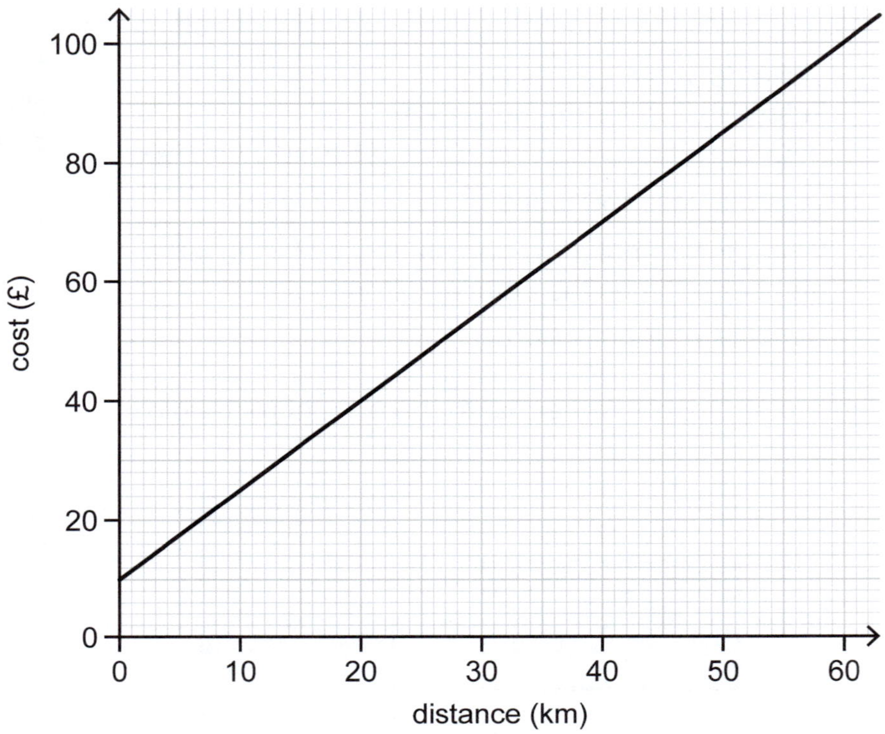


For each delivery, there is a fixed cost plus a charge for the distance.

**a)** How much is the fixed cost? **(1 mark)**

Max makes two deliveries in February.

The distance of one delivery is 30 km more than the distance of the other delivery.

**b)** Work out the difference between the two delivery costs. **(2 marks)**

> Choose two distances that are 30 km apart.
> For example, 0 km and 30 km.
> Find the cost for each distance.

**A10.** Ben, Kirsten and Mahalia sell books in the market.

Mahalia sells $x$ books.

Kirsten sells 2 more books than Mahalia.

Ben sells twice as many books as Mahalia.

**a)** Find and simplify expression, in terms of $x$, for the total number of books the three children sell. **(2 marks)**

Ben, Kirsten and Mahalia sell 70 books in total.

**b)** Find the number of books that each child sells. **(3 marks)**

## Algebra Set B

**B1.** Oliver has 15 cherries.
Hannah has 20 cherries.
Oliver gives Hannah $2x$ cherries.
Oliver then eats 5 of his cherries.
Hannah then eats half of her cherries.

**a)** Write an expression, in terms of $x$, for the number of cherries that Oliver now has. **(1 mark)**

**b)** Write an expression, in terms of $x$, for the number of cherries that Hannah now has. **(1 mark)**

Hannah now has 13 cherries.

**c)** Find the number of cherries that Oliver gave to Hannah. **(2 marks)**

**B2.** Stuart is $x$ years old.
Jake is four times as old as Stuart.
Isabella is 9 years older than Stuart.

**a)** Write an expression, in terms of $x$, for the mean of their ages. **(3 marks)**

> To work out the mean, add up the three ages and then divide by 3.

The mean of their ages is 17 years old.

**b)** Work out the range of their ages. **(3 marks)**

> To work out the range:
> - First, set your expression from part **a)** equal to 17, then solve for $x$.
> - Then, work out each child's age and subtract the lowest from the highest.

**B3.** In the diagram, all measurements are given in centimetres.
All angles are right angles.

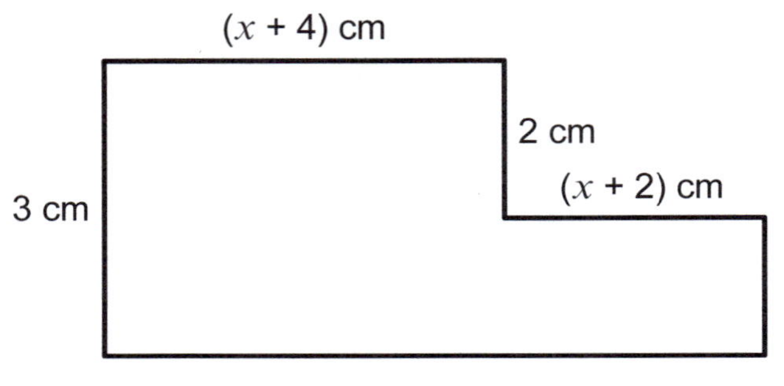


not drawn accurately

**a)** Show that the area of the shape can be written as $2(2x + 7)$. **(3 marks)**

> Split the shape into two rectangles.

The area of the shape is 51 cm$^2$.

**b)** Work out the perimeter of the shape. **(3 marks)**

**B4.** The diagram shows shape A.
All measurements are in centimetres.

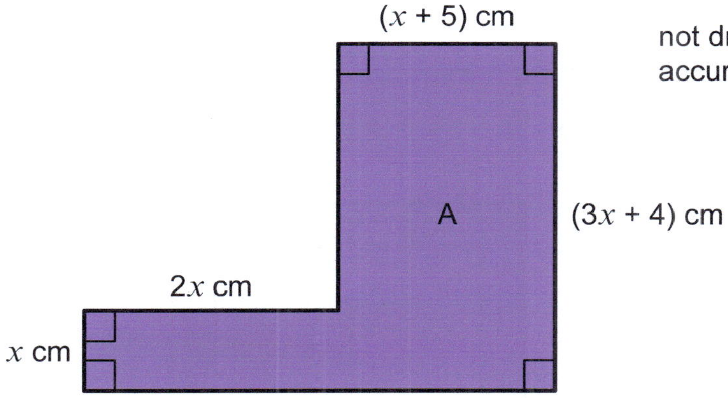


not drawn accurately

**a)** Find an expression, in terms of $x$, for the perimeter of shape A. **(2 marks)**

> This is similar to Question B3.

An equilateral triangle B has the same perimeter as shape A.

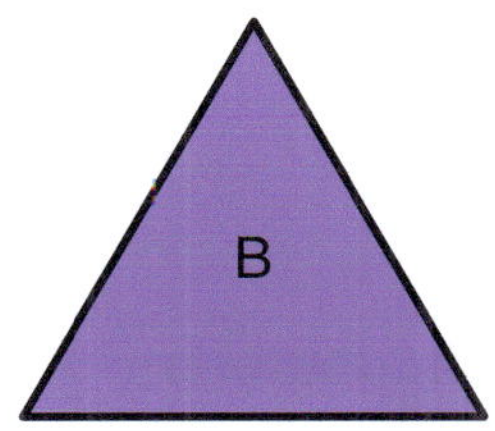


**b)** Find an expression, in terms of $x$, for the length of one side of this triangle. **(2 marks)**

> All the sides in an equilateral triangle are the same length.

**B5.** Class 11A sold $x$ cupcakes at the school fair.
Class 11B sold twice as many cupcakes as Class 11A.
Class 11C sold 13 more cupcakes than Class 11B.

**a)** Write an expression, in terms of $x$, for the total number of cupcakes that all 3 classes sold. **(2 marks)**

The total number of cupcakes sold by all three classes was 108.

**b)** How many cupcakes did each class sell? **(3 marks)**

> Make the answer from part **a)** equal to 108.

**B6.** Here is a rectangle made of card.

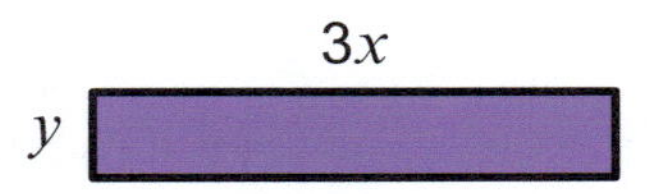


The measurements in the diagram are in centimetres.
Aisha fits four of these rectangles together to make a frame, as shown in the diagram.

The perimeter of the **outside** of the frame is $P$ cm.

**a)** Show that $P = 12x + 4y$ **(2 marks)**

The perimeter of the inside of the frame is $K$ cm.

**b)** Show that $K = 12x - 4y$ **(2 marks)**

**B7.** ABC is a triangle.
All angles are measured in degrees.

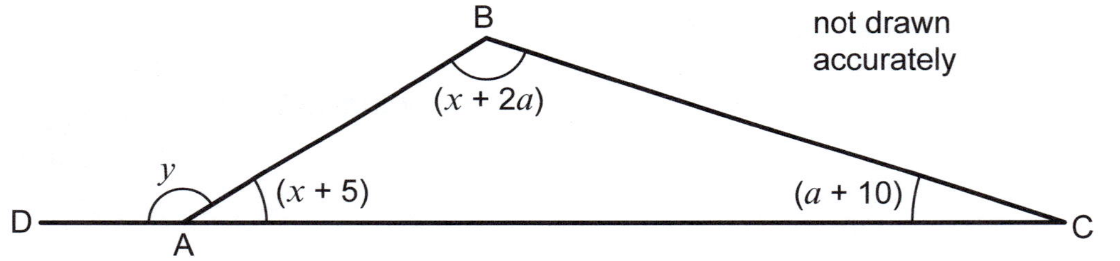


**a)** Show that $2x + 3a = 165°$ **(2 marks)**

What do the angles in a triangle add up to?

**b)** Show that $y = 175° - x$ **(2 marks)**

The angles at a point on a straight line add up to 180°.

**B8.** Lira is attempting to solve the following equation.

$(x + 2)(x + 3) = (x - 1)(x - 5)$

Her incorrect solution is given below.

$$
\begin{aligned}
(x + 2)(x + 3) &= (x - 1)(x - 5) \\
x^2 + 2x + 3x + 6 &= x^2 - x - 5x + 5 \\
x^2 + 5x + 6 &= x^2 - 4x + 5 \\
5x + 6 &= -4x + 5 \\
9x + 6 &= 5 \\
9x &= -1 \\
x &= -9
\end{aligned}
$$

**a)** Identify two mistakes Lira makes. **(2 marks)**

**b)** Write down the correct working and solution. **(1 mark)**

**B9.** Toby thinks of a number $x$.
He multiplies this number by 12 and then subtracts 7.
The result is 101.
Find the value of $x$. **(2 marks)**

**B10.** The hexagon ABCDEF has a vertical line of symmetry.

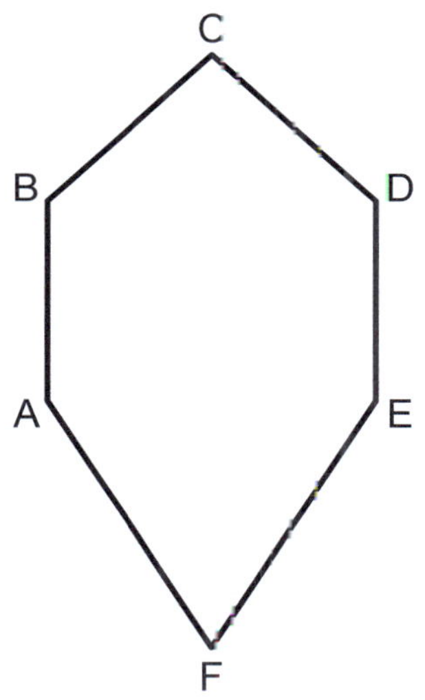


> As the hexagon has a line of symmetry, the right-hand side = left-hand side.
> $BC = CD$, $AB = DE$ and $AF = FE$

$AB = 3x - 2$
$BC = 2x - 3$
$AF = 2x + 6$

All the measurements are given in centimetres.
The perimeter of the hexagon is 86 cm.

**a)** Show that $14x + 2 = 86$ **(3 marks)**

**b)** Find the value of $x$. **(2 marks)**

## Algebra Set C

**C1.** Josh thinks of a number $y$.
He subtracts 4 then adds 13.
The result equals two times the original number $y$.

**a)** Show that $y + 9 = 2y$ **(2 marks)**

**b)** What number is Josh thinking of? **(1 mark)**

**C2.** Elias has $x$ cards.
Arthur has twice as many cards as Elias.
Charlie has 9 more cards than Arthur.
They have a total of 64 cards.

**a)** Show that $5x + 9 = 64$ **(3 marks)**

**b)** Work out the number of cards Elias has. **(2 marks)**

**C3.** Esme sells three boxes of oranges at the market.
There are $x$ oranges in box A.
There are $(3x + 2)$ oranges in box B.
There are $(2x - 4)$ oranges in box C.
There are 160 oranges in total in all the three boxes.
Work out the number of oranges in each box. **(4 marks)**

**C4.** Marion is 4 years older than Asif.
Teresa is 2 years younger than Asif.
The total of their ages is 53 years.
Asif is $x$ years old.
Work out the age of Asif. **(4 marks)**

**C5.** MNP is a triangle.
The perimeter of the triangle is 38 cm.

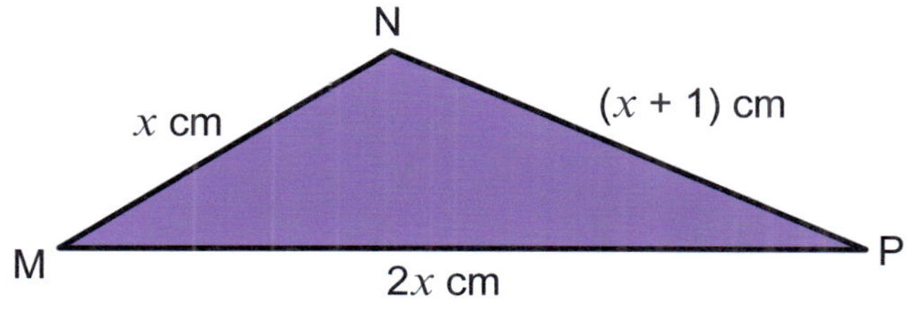


**a)** Show that $4x + 1 = 38$ **(2 marks)**

**b)** Work out the length of the longest side of the triangle. **(2 marks)**

**C6.** Maisy has the same number of shells as Harry.
Maisy gives 18 of her shells to Harry.
Harry now has 3 times as many shells as Maisy.
Work out the total number of shells Maisy and Harry have. **(3 marks)**

> Suppose Maisy and Harry each begin with $x$ shells.
> Set up and solve an equation to find $x$.

**C7.** The diagram shows a trapezium.

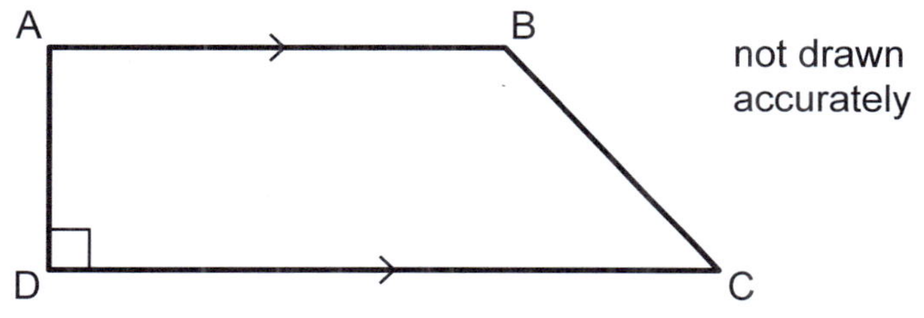


AD = $x$ cm.
BC is 1 cm longer than AD.
AB is twice the length of AD.
DC is 5 cm longer than AB.
The perimeter of the trapezium is 78 cm.

**a)** Show that $3x + 3 = 39$ **(3 marks)**

**b)** Work out the length of AD. **(2 marks)**

**C8.** ABC is a triangle.

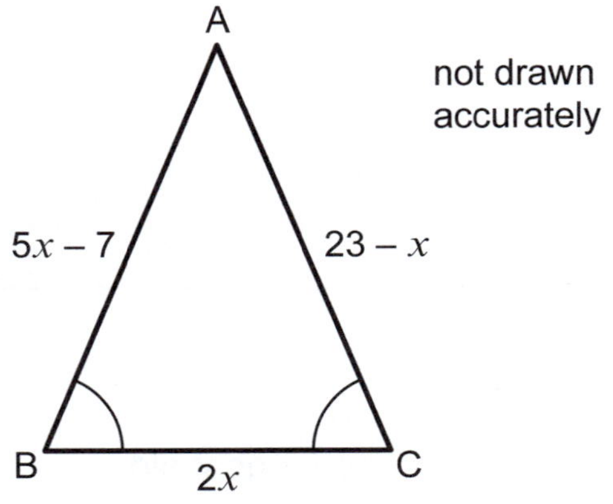


angle ABC = angle BCA

The length of side AB is $(5x - 7)$ cm.

The length of side AC is $(23 - x)$ cm.

The length of side BC is $2x$ cm.

Work out the perimeter of the triangle.

Give your answer in centimetres. **(5 marks)**

> Because angle ABC = angle BCA, you know that triangle ABC is isosceles.
> What can you say about the lengths of AB and AC?
> Use this to set up and solve an equation to find the value of $x$.

**C9.** Holly is $x$ years old.

Leon is twice as old as Holly.

Talya is 3 years younger than Leon.

The sum of all their ages is 52 years.

**a)** Show that $5x - 3 = 52$ **(3 marks)**

**b)** Work out the age of Talya. **(3 marks)**

**C10.** Keaumont School sent $x$ students to a Science revision day.

Oak College sent twice as many students as Keaumont School.

Mandringham School sent 7 fewer students than Oak College.

Each student paid £15 for the revision day.

The students paid a total of £1170

Work out how many students were sent by Oak College to the revision day.

You must show all your working. **(5 marks)**

## Algebra Set D

**D1.** Ishani and Georgia are selling pens in a school shop.
They sell boxes of pens, and single pens.
There are $x$ pens in each box of pens
Ishani sells 6 boxes of pens and 4 single pens.
Georgia sells 2 boxes of pens and 11 single pens.
Ishani sells two times as many pens as Georgia sells.
Work out the number of pens in each box.
You must show all your working. **(4 marks)**

**D2.** Evie has saved her pocket money.
Maya has saved twice as much money as Evie.
Alex has saved £18
Evie, Maya and Alex have saved a total of £87
How much money has Maya saved? **(3 marks)**

**D3.** Konnie has a 5-sided spinner.
The sides of the spinner are numbered 1, 2, 3, 4 and 5.
The spinner is biased.
The table shows the probabilities of the spinner landing on each number.
The probability that the spinner will land on 2 is $x$.
The probability that the spinner will land on 3 is twice the probability that the spinner lands on 2.

| **Number** | 1 | 2 | 3 | 4 | 5 |
|---|---|---|---|---|---|
| **Probability** | 0.1 | $x$ | | 0.15 | |

**a)** Find an expression, in terms of $x$, for the probability that the spinner will land on 3.
Give your answer in its simplest form. **(1 mark)**

**b)** Find an expression, in terms of $x$, for the probability that the spinner will land on 5.
Give your answer in its simplest form. **(3 marks)**

Probabilities always add up to 1.

**c)** The probability of landing on 5 is 0.21
Work out the value of $x$. **(3 marks)**

**D4.** The diagram shows a rectangle.
The line DA splits the rectangle into two trapeziums.

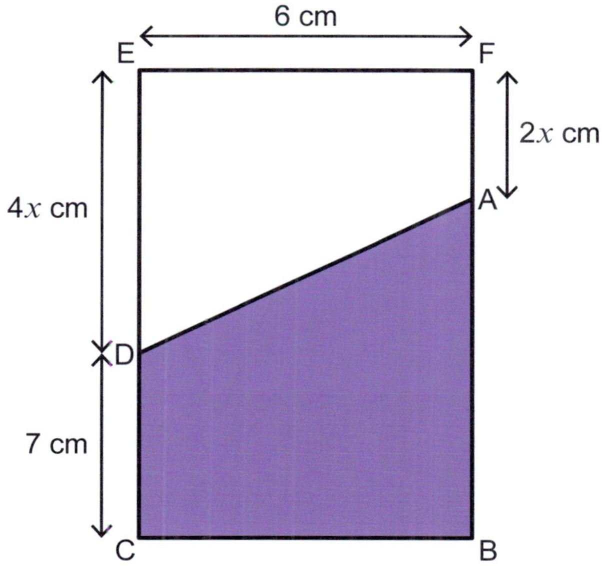


The area of trapezium ABCD = 90 cm$^2$.

**a)** Show that $2x + 14 = 30$ **(3 marks)**

**b)** Find the length of EC. **(3 marks)**

Find the area of the trapezium. Make it equal to 90 cm$^2$.

**D5.** CDEF is a straight line.

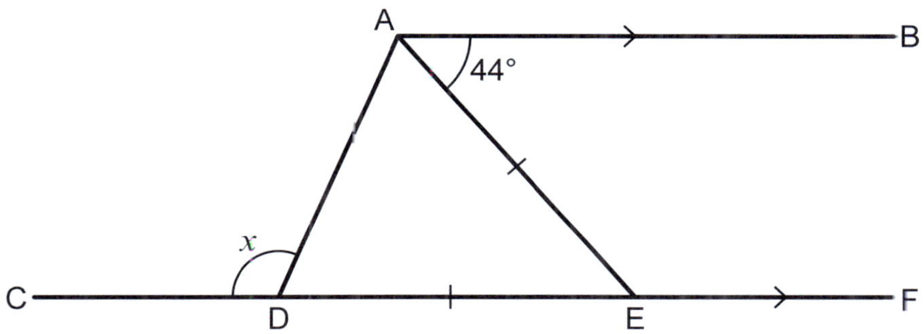


AB is parallel to CF.
DE = AE
Calculate the size of angle CDA.
You must give reasons for your answer. **(4 marks)**

Which angle in triangle AED is equal to 44°?

**D6.** ABCD is a kite.

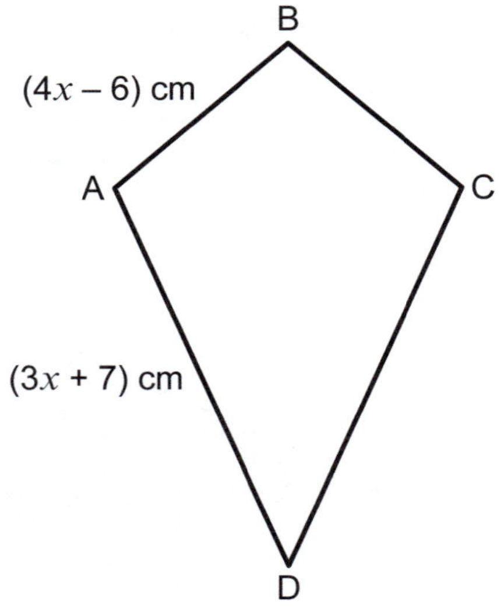


AB = $(4x - 6)$ cm
AD = $(3x + 7)$ cm
Amelia says that $x$ could be 1 cm.

**a)** Explain why Amelia cannot be correct. **(1 mark)**

The kite has a perimeter of 100 cm.

**b)** Find the value of $x$. **(3 marks)**

**D7.** The diagram shows a pentagon.
The pentagon has a vertical line of symmetry.

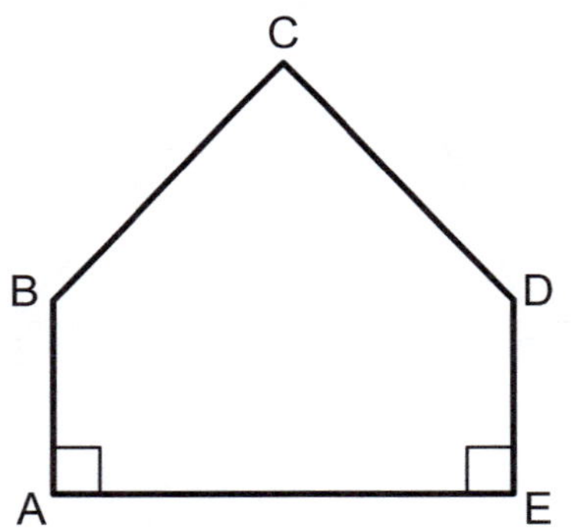


AE = $4x$
AB = $x + 2$
BC = 3 × AB
All these measurements are given in centimetres.
The perimeter of the pentagon is 112 cm.

**a)** Show that $3x + 4 = 28$ **(3 marks)**

**b)** Find the length of AE. **(3 marks)**

**D8.** **a)** $x$ and $y$ are even different numbers.
Give an example to show that the value of $3(x + y)$ is a multiple of 6. **(2 marks)**

**b)** $x$ and $y$ are two consecutive odd numbers.
Give an example to show that the value of $x + y$ will be a multiple of 4. **(2 marks)**

> **Consecutive odd numbers** are two odd numbers that are separated by just one even number. For example, 7 and 9 are consecutive odd numbers.

**D9.** The area of rectangle ABCD is 50 cm².

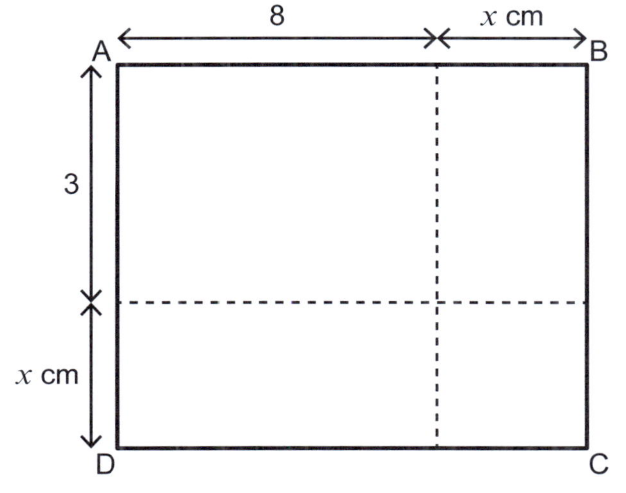


Show that $x^2 + 11x = 26$ **(3 marks)**

**D10.** Here is a triangle.

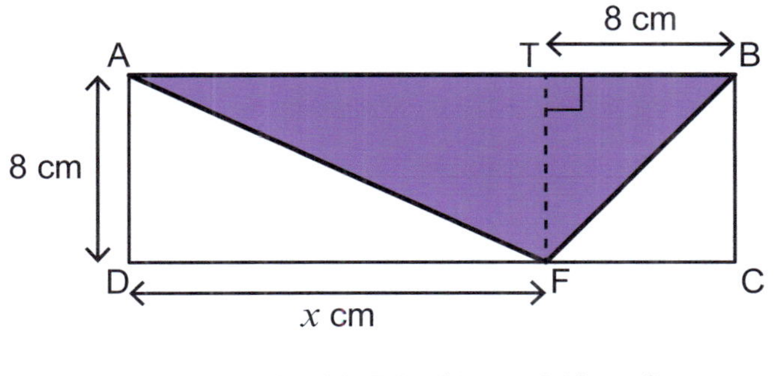


Show that the area of the triangle ABF is $(4x + 32)$ cm². **(3 marks)**

> Think of the triangle as being upside down. AB is the base, and TF is the height.

## Algebra Set E

**E1.**

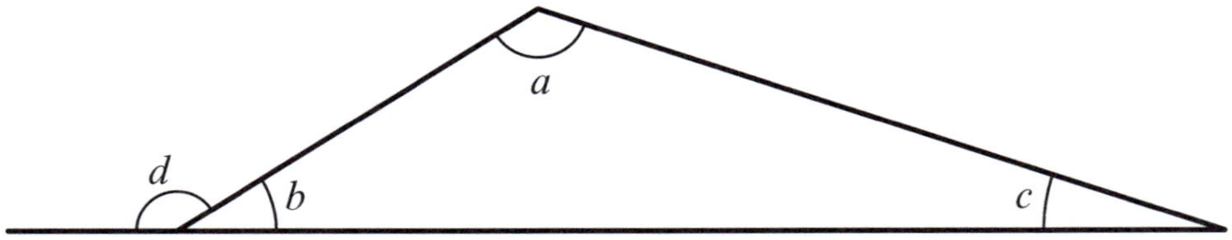


Angle $a$ is three times the size of angle $b$.
Angle $c$ is half the size of angle $b$.
Find the size of angle $d$. Give your answer in degrees. **(3 marks)**

> Write all the angles in terms of angle $b$. What is angle $a$ equal to? What about angle $c$?
> Remember that the sum of the angles in a triangle is 180°, and the sum of the angles on a straight line is 180°.

**E2.** You are told that $6x + 14 = 140$
Find the values of:

- **a)** $6x + 4$ **(2 marks)**
- **b)** $3x + 7$ **(2 marks)**
- **c)** $12x + 28$ **(2 marks)**
- **d)** $12x + 8$ **(2 marks)**

> You don't have to find $x$.
> For example, in part **a)** start with $6x + 14 = 140$. What do you need to do to both sides to get $6x + 4$ on the left-hand side?

**E3.** You are told that $4x - 2 = 50$
Find the values of:

- **a)** $2x - 1$ **(2 marks)**
- **b)** $4x + 5$ **(2 marks)**
- **c)** $4x - 1$ **(2 marks)**
- **d)** $8x - 4$ **(2 marks)**

> You don't have to find $x$.
> For example, in part **a)** start with $4x - 2 = 50$. What do you need to do to both sides to get $2x - 1$ on the left-hand side?

**E4.** A is the point with coordinates $(a, 1)$.
B is the point with coordinates $(1, 7)$.
The gradient of the line AB = 3.
Find the value of $a$. **(4 marks)**

> The gradient of a line = $\frac{\text{change in } y}{\text{change in } x} = \frac{y_2 - y_1}{x_2 - x_1}$

**E5.** A is the point with coordinates $(x, 2x)$.
B is the point with coordinates $(4x, 3x)$.
Show that the gradient of the line segment AB is $\frac{1}{3}$ **(3 marks)**

**E6.** A circle is cut from a square piece of paper.

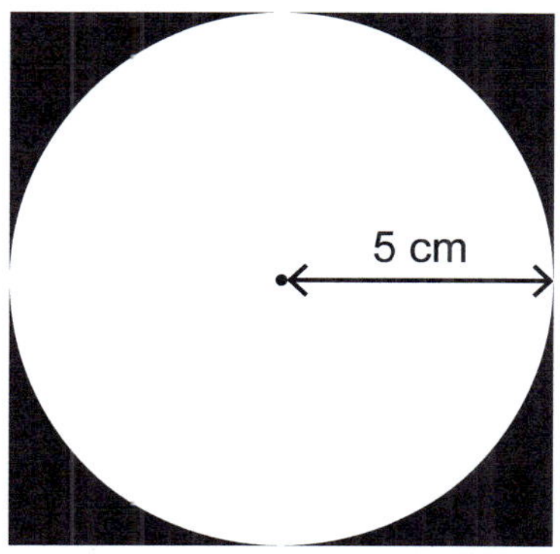


The radius of the circle is 5 cm.
Show that the remaining area of paper can be written as $25(4 - \pi)$ cm$^2$.
**(4 marks)**

> What is the length of a side of the square?
> What is the area of the square?

**E7.** AB is parallel to CD.

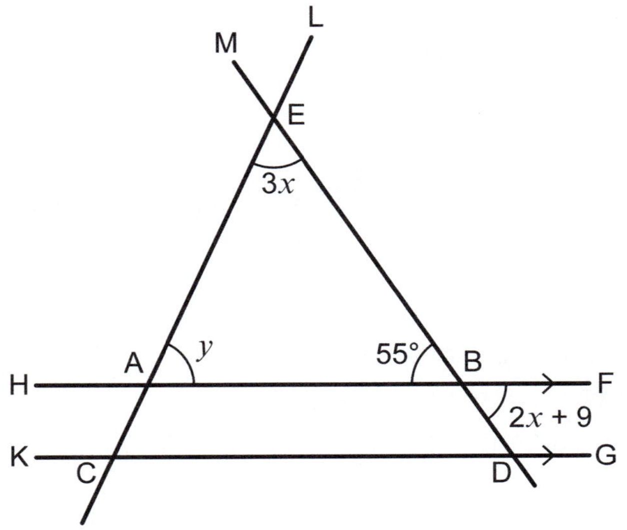


**a)** Work out $x$.
Give a reason for each stage of your working. **(3 marks)**

**b)** Work out $y$.
Give a reason for each stage of your working. **(3 marks)**

**E8.** ABC is a triangle.
ACD is a straight line.

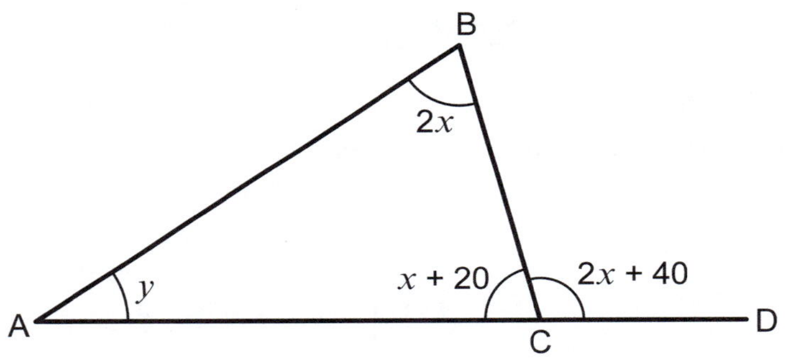


**a)** Find the value of $x$.
Give a reason for each stage of your working. **(3 marks)**

**b)** Find the value of $y$.
Give a reason for each stage of your working. **(2 marks)**

**E9.** The diagram shows a pentagon. All angles are measured in degrees.

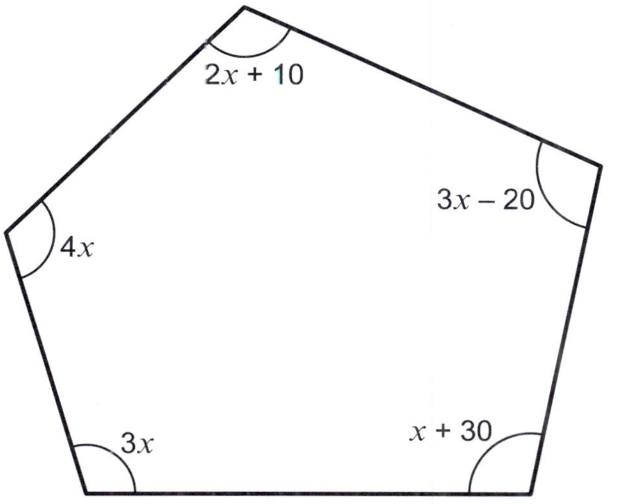


**a)** Calculate the value of $x$. **(3 marks)**

**b)** Hence, work out the size of the largest angle in the pentagon. **(2 marks)**

What do the interior angles in a pentagon add up to?

**E10.** Orlaigh scores $x$ marks in a test.

Maya scores 12 more marks than Orlaigh.

Arthur scores twice as many marks as Maya.

**a)** Write an expression, in terms of $x$, for the total number of marks scored by the three students. Simplify your answer. **(2 marks)**

The total number of marks scored by all the students is 236.

**b)** How many marks did each child score? **(4 marks)**

# End of Chapter Notes

You could try and complete the 10 questions in each set, in a single study session. This may help with exam practice and keeping the focus going even when the questions are challenging.

| |
|---|
| 1. |
| 2. |
| 3. |

Write 3 things you feel you need to keep an eye on.

| |
|---|
| 1. |
| 2. |
| 3. |

Write 3 common mistakes that either you or your friends may make.

You could write specific mistakes or whole questions that you feel are easy to make a mistake on.

| |
|---|
| 1. |
| 2. |
| 3. |

## Well done for completing this chapter!

# Chapter 2
# Ratio and Proportion

*"The cold water does not get any warmer if you jump late." – James Hallahan*

Worked Solutions

# Ratio and proportion: Worked examples

**Here are five worked examples to get you started on this topic.**

- **Look at each example in turn.**
- **Can you do the question independently?**
- **If not, go over it slowly and work through the solution.**

## Worked example 1

A recipe to make 24 fairy cakes requires the following ingredients:

300 g flour    270 g butter    230 g sugar    4 eggs

**a)** Work out the amount of flour that is required to make 12 fairy cakes. **(2 marks)**

**b)** Work out the amount of sugar that is required to make 60 fairy cakes. **(2 marks)**

### Solution

**a)** Flour for 12 cakes = 300 ÷ 2 **(1 mark)**

= 150 g **(1 mark)**

12 is half of 24, so halve the amount of flour needed.

**b) Method 1**

12 is a factor of both 24 and 60.

÷2    ×5

| **Number of cakes** | 24 cakes | 12 cakes | 60 cakes |
|---|---|---|---|
| **Amount of sugar** | 230 g | 115 g | 575 g |

÷2    ×5

**(1 mark for dividing by 2)**

**(1 mark for multiplying by 5)**

**Method 2**

24 × 2 = 48

48 + 12 = 60 **(1 mark)**

First, double the amount of sugar for 24 cakes, then add half again.

230 g × 2 = 460 g

$\frac{1}{2}$ of 230 g = 115 g

460 g + 115 g = 575 g sugar **(1 mark)**

## Worked example 2

A machine contains two discs, A and B.

Disc A turns twice when disc B turns 5 times.

When disc B turns 40 times, how many times does disc A turn? **(2 marks)**

### Solution

| | A | B | |
|---|---|---|---|
| ×8 | 2 times | 5 times | ×8 |
| | ? | 40 times | |

Number of turns on disc A = 2 × 8 **(1 mark)**

= 16 times **(1 mark)**

If two quantities are in direct proportion, if you multiply one quantity by a number then you have to multiply the other quantity by the same number.

### Worked example 3

A machine in a factory prepares 12 boxes in 30 seconds.
Work out how long the machine needs to prepare 20 boxes. **(3 marks)**

### Solution

2 divides into 12, 20 and 30

| | | | |
|---|---|---|---|
| | 12 boxes | 30 seconds | |
| ÷6 | | | ÷6 |
| | 2 boxes | 5 seconds | |
| ×10 | | | ×10 |
| | 20 boxes | 50 seconds | |

It takes 50 seconds to prepare 12 boxes. **(1 mark)**

If two quantities are in direct proportion, if you multiply one quantity by a number then you have to multiply the other quantity by the same number.

### Worked example 4

The ratio of the number of blue pens to the number of green pens is 3 : 7
The ratio of the number of green pens to the number of red pens is 2 : 5
Work out the ratio of **blue pens** : **green pens** : **red pens** **(3 marks)**

### Solution

Make the number of green pens 14 in both ratios.

| | Blue | : | Green | | | Green | : | Red | |
|---|---|---|---|---|---|---|---|---|---|
| | 3 | : | 7 | | | 2 | : | 5 | |
| ×2 | | | | ×2 | ×7 | | | | ×7 |
| | 6 | : | 14 | | | 14 | : | 35 | |

**(1 mark)** **(1 mark)**

Both ratios contain green pens. Make the number of green pens the same in both ratios.

So ratio of **blue pens** : **green pens** : **red pens**
= 6 : 14 : 35 **(1 mark)**

When the number of green pens in both ratios is the same, you can write the ratio of all three colours.

## Worked example 5

The ratio of students who study Geography GCSE to the number of students that study History GCSE is 3 : 8. No-one studies both.

There are 20 more students that study History than Geography.

Work out the total number of students that study History and Geography. **(3 marks)**

## Solution

**Method 1**

The ratio has 3 + 8 = 11 parts in total. **(1 mark)**

5 parts of the ratio represents 20 students.

20 ÷ 5 = 4 so 1 part of the ratio represents 4 students. **(1 mark)**

total number of students = 11 × 4 = 44 **(1 mark)**

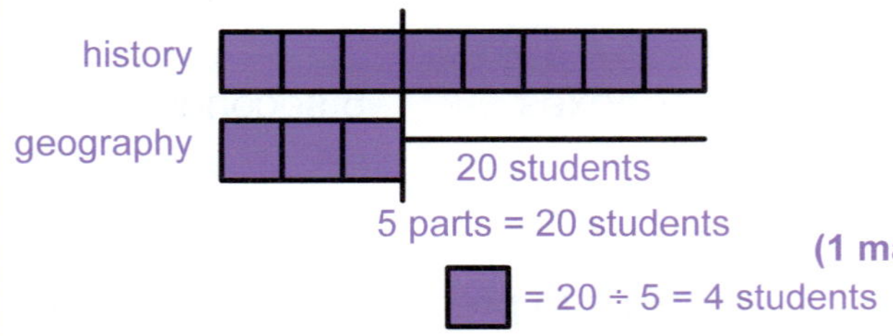


**(1 mark)**

**Method 2**

Let the number that study Geography = $3x$

Then the number that study History = $8x$

Difference between history and geography is $8x - 3x = 5x$

There are 20 more students that study History than Geography, so

$5x = 20$ ↓Now divide both sides by 5

$x = 4$ **(1 mark)**

Geography = 3 × 4 = 12 students

History = 8 × 4 = 32 students **(1 mark)**

total is 12 + 32 = 44 students **(1 mark)**

This method uses algebra.

You do not know how many students study each subject, but you know the numbers are in the ratio 3 : 8

So you can express the number that study geography as $3 \times x$ for some whole number $x$.

The number that study history can then be written as $8 \times x$.

Now try each set of questions.

You might want to create a table like this in your exercise book to record your progress.

You could try and complete the 10 questions in each set, in a single study session.

This may help with exam practice and keeping the focus going even when the questions are challenging.

| Study session | Question set | Tick when completed | How do I feel about these questions? Difficult – I need to improve my understanding of … |
|---|---|---|---|
| 1 | A | | |
| 2 | B | | |
| 3 | C | | |
| 4 | D | | |
| 5 | E | | |

Remember, there is no 'quick fix' when problem solving. If you are stuck, this is a good thing. It means you are being challenged and you are learning.

Worked Solutions are here **https://www.oliviapresspublishers.com**

**All diagrams** in this chapter are not drawn accurately unless otherwise stated.

**GCSE students** can use a calculator unless they see this symbol 

**International GCSE students** can use a calculator in all the questions.

## Ratio and proportion Set A

**A1.** ABC is a right-angled triangle.

The ratio size of angle CBA : size of angle BAC is 3 : 2

Work out the size of the smallest angle. **(3 marks)**

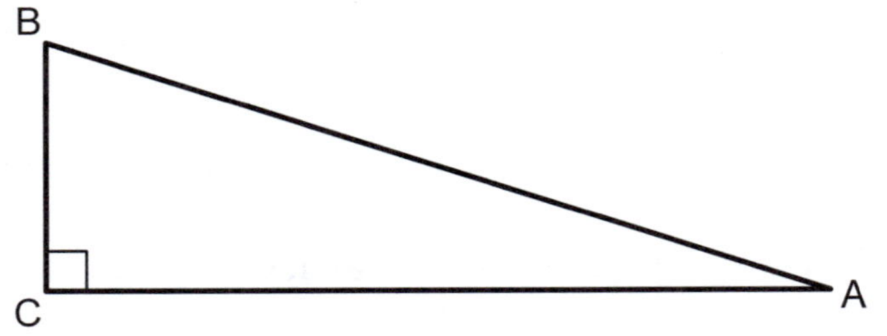


**A2.** A football team played 72 matches last year.

The ratio of matches lost : matches won : matches drawn was 2 : 3 : 13.

How many matches did the team win? **(3 marks)**

**A3.** The ratio of the angles in a triangle is 2 : 3 : 1.

Amy says that the triangle is a right-angled triangle.

Is Amy correct?

Show your working clearly to justify your answer. **(3 marks)**

**A4.** The diagram shows triangle ABC.

ADB is a straight line.

The ratio of angle DCB : angle ACD is 3 : 2

Work out the size of angle BDC. **(4 marks)**

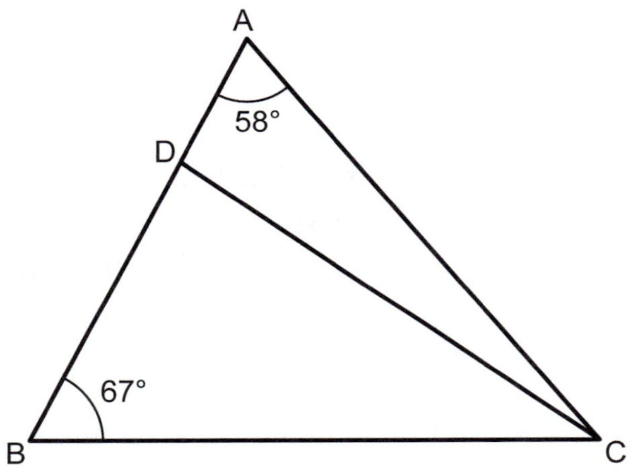


**A5.** The diagram shows isosceles triangle BCD.

BC = BD

ABC is a straight line.

The ratio of angle ABD : angle CBD is 7 : 2

Work out the size of angle BCD. **(3 marks)**

What do the angles at a point in a straight line add up to?

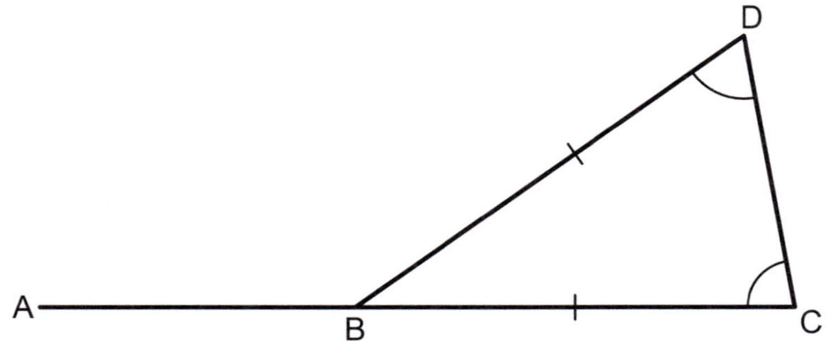

**A6.** Iris has three times as many cousins as Jojo.
Jojo has half as many cousins as Edward.
Work out the ratio of the number of
Jojo's cousins : Edward's cousins : Iris's cousins **(2 marks)**

**A7.** There are 80 students in the school bus.
They are from Year 7, Year 8 and Year 9.
One quarter of the students are from Year 7.
The number of Year 8 students is four times the number of the Year 9 students.
The ratio
number of Year 8 students : number of Year 7 students
is $n:1$.
Work out the value of $n$.
You must show how you get your answer. **(4 marks)**

> Read the question slowly.
> Find the number of Year 7 students first.

**A8.** The mass of an apple is half the mass of an orange.
The mass of a melon is three times as much as the mass of an orange.
Work out the ratio of apple mass : melon mass.
Give your answer in the form $1:n$ **(3 marks)**

> Let apple mass be 1 part.
> How many parts will the orange mass be?

**A9.** The number of days ($d$) it takes to decorate a house is given by

$$d = \frac{480}{N}$$

where $N$ is the number of people working.
There are 16 people working for company A.
There are 12 people working for company B.
How many fewer days does it take company A to decorate a house than it takes company B?
**(3 marks)**

**A10.** It takes six builders 8 days to build an office.

**a)** Calculate how long it will take one builder to build the office. **(1 mark)**

**b)** Calculate how long it will take four builders to build the office. **(1 mark)**

## Ratio and proportion Set B

**B1.** It takes three decorators 4 days to paint six rooms.
How long will four decorators take to paint 12 rooms? **(3 marks)**

**B2.** It takes 1 hour 20 minutes to fill a paddling pool using water from three taps.

**a)** Work out the time it takes to fill the pool when:

**i)** only one tap is used **(2 marks)**

**ii)** four taps are used. **(2 marks)**

**b)** State one assumption you made in working out your answer to part **a) i)**. **(1 mark)**

**B3.** There are 495 coins in a jar.
The jar contains only 50p coins, 20p coins and £1 coins.
The ratio of 50p coins to 20p coins to £1 coins is $6:7:2$
Work out the total value of the 495 coins. **(4 marks)**

**B4.** Hayley and Joseph have a total of 24 shells.
The ratio of the number of Hayley's shells to the number of Joseph's shells is $3:5$
Joseph gives Hayley some shells.
The ratio of the number of Hayley's shells to the number of Joseph's shells is now $3:1$
How many shells does Joseph give Hayley?
You must show all your working. **(4 marks)**

**B5.** A pattern is made of circle tiles and square tiles.
$\frac{3}{7}$ of the tiles are circles.

**a)** Work out the ratio of squares to circles. **(1 mark)**

$\frac{1}{2}$ of the squares are grey.

$\frac{1}{3}$ of the circles are grey.

The rest of the shapes are white.

**b)** Write down the ratio of grey shapes to white shapes. **(3 marks)**

**B6.** On a farm:

- the ratio of **number of cows : number of sheep** is $5:6$
- the ratio of **number of sheep : number of pigs** is $8:5$

There are 30 pigs on the farm.
Work out the number of cows on the farm. **(3 marks)**

**B7.** A school sports club is made up of students from Year 9 and Year 10. Students play either hockey or football. No-one plays both.

There are 28 students who play hockey from Year 9.

45% of the students from Year 10 play hockey.

There are 33 students who play football from Year 10.

The ratio of **hockey players : football players** in the club is 5 : 4

Work out the total number of students in the club. **(5 marks)**

**B8.** A company has 240 cars and vans.

The ratio of **number of cars : number of vans** is 3 : 7

Each car and each van uses either electricity, petrol or diesel.

$\frac{1}{8}$ of the vans use electricity.

The ratio of **vans that use petrol : vans that use diesel** is 1 : 2.

Work out the number of vans that use diesel. **(5 marks)**

**B9.** A shop sells packs of yellow highlighters and packs of orange highlighters.

There are:

- 7 highlighters in each pack of yellow highlighters
- 8 highlighters in each pack of orange highlighters

On Monday, the ratio **number of packs of yellow highlighters sold : number of packs of orange highlighters sold** is 2 : 3

A total of 228 highlighters were sold.

Work out the number of orange highlighters sold. **(4 marks)**

> Start by letting the number of packs of yellow highlighters sold be $2x$.
>
> A yellow pack contains 7 highlighters, so the total number or yellow highlighters sold is $2x \times 7$.
>
> Write a similar expression for orange highlighters.

**B10.** A box contains blue pens, green pens and red pens.

The ratio of the number of blue pens to the number of green pens is 3 : 5.

The ratio of the number of green pens to the number of red pens is 2 : 7.

There are fewer than 105 pens in the box.

What is the greatest possible number of red pens in the box? **(4 marks)**

## Ratio and proportion Set C

**C1.** A rectangle is made from small coloured square tiles.
There are yellow tiles, blue tiles and red tiles.
The ratio **yellow tiles : blue tiles : red tiles** is 2 : 5 : 1
The are 24 more blue tiles than yellow tiles.
How many red tiles are there? **(3 marks)**

**C2.** The diagram shows a cuboid.

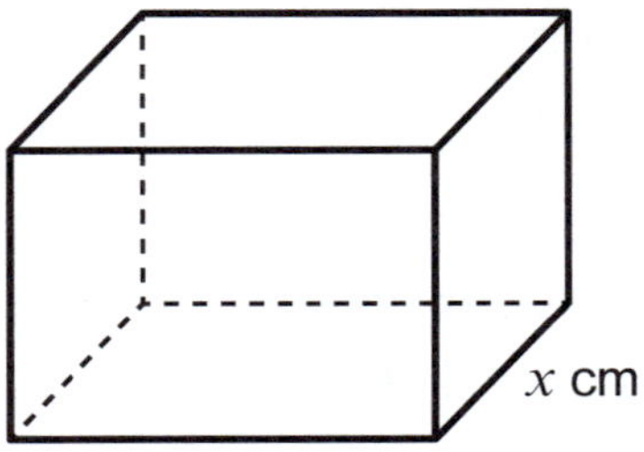


not drawn accurately

The width of the cuboid is $x$ cm.
The ratio **width : length : height** is 1 : 3 : 2
The volume of the cuboid is 48 $cm^3$.
Work out the value of $x$. **(3 marks)**

**C3.** Jacob and Sasha are going to drive for a total time of 4 hours 30 minutes.
They are going to share the driving so that the ratio of
**time Jacob drives : time Sasha drives** is 1 : 2.
Sasha says, 'If we both drive at an average speed of 60 km/h,
I will drive 100 km more than Jacob.'
Is Sasha correct?
You must show how you get your answer. **(5 marks)**

**C4.** A bag contains only red cubes and blue cubes.
The ratio of the number of red cubes to the number of blue cubes is 3 : 5
There are 240 blue cubes in the bag.
Nic takes 24 red cubes out of the bag.
How many blue cubes does he need to take out so that the ratio remains 3 : 5? **(5 marks)**

**C5.** Johan has either small boxes, medium boxes and large boxes.
The ratios of the number of:

- small boxes : medium boxes = 2 : 5
- medium boxes : large boxes = 4 : 7

Johan has more than 150 boxes in total.
What is the least possible number of large boxes that he could have? **(4 marks)**

**C6.** Yusuf makes some bird tables.
To make 6 bird tables Yusuf needs:

- 9 metres of wood
- 6 wooden trays
- 36 nails.

Write out a list of materials Yusuf would need to make:

**a)** 15 bird tables **(3 marks)**

**b)** 7 bird tables. **(3 marks)**

**C7.** It takes four builders 9 days to build a conservatory.

**a)** Find the number of days it would take one builder to build the conservatory on his own. **(1 mark)**

**b)** Find the number of days it would take 12 builders to build the conservatory. **(2 marks)**

**C8.** Archie, Owen and Jo have saved £98 between them.
Archie has saved half as much as Jo.
Jo has saved 4 times as much as Owen.
How much money has Jo saved? **(3 marks)**

**C9.** Teresa needs 80 g of sugar to make 12 cookies.
She also needs two times as much butter as sugar.
Teresa is going to make 60 cookies.
She buys the butter in 200 g packs.
Work out the number of packs of butter she buys. **(3 marks)**

**C10.** Here is a list of ingredients for making 16 flapjacks.

| Ingredients for 16 flapjacks |
|---|
| 120 g butter |
| 140 g brown sugar |
| 300 g oats |
| 2 tablespoons syrup |

Jenny wants to make 24 flapjacks.
Work out how much of each of the ingredients she needs. **(4 marks)**

## Ratio and proportion Set D

**D1.** Here is the list of ingredients for making 30 chocolate chip cookies.

| Ingredients for 30 cookies |
|---|
| 200 g butter |
| 100 g caster sugar |
| 275 g plain flour |
| 75 g chocolate chips |

Lucas has the following ingredients:

- 900 g butter
- 1000 g caster sugar
- 1100 g plain flour
- 225 g chocolate chips.

Work out the greatest number of cookies Lucas can make.
You must show your working. **(3 marks)**

> Even if Lucas has enough sugar to make 300 biscuits, it doesn't necessarily mean he can make 300 biscuits.
> The greatest number of biscuits he can make is the number of biscuits that he has all the ingredients for.

**D2.** Here are the ingredients needed to make 16 biscuits:

| Ingredients for 16 biscuits |
|---|
| 200 g of butter |
| 150 g of sugar |
| 300 g of flour |

Anya has:

- 500 g of butter
- 300 g of sugar
- 625 g of flour.

Work out the greatest number of biscuits Anya can make. **(3 marks)**

**D3.** Lila is going to use these instructions to make a lemonade:

*Mix 5 parts of water with 2 parts of lemon concentrate.*

Lila has 1 litre of water and 500 ml of lemon concentrate.
Work out the greatest amount of lemonade Lila can make. **(3 marks)**

**D4.** A builder is making concrete.
The builder uses:

- 90 kg of cement
- 180 kg of sand
- 540 kg of stone

**a)** Work out the ratio of cement : sand : stone in its simplest form. **(2 marks)**

Cement, sand and stone are sold in bags.

| 1 bag cement | 1 bag sand | 1 bag stone |
|---|---|---|
| 40 kg | 35 kg | 60 kg |

The builder has:

- 5 bags of cement
- 20 bags of sand
- 20 bags of stone

**b)** Work out the largest mass of concrete the builder can make.
Give your answer in kg. **(5 marks)**

**D5.** There are 120 cans of drinks on a shelf.
Each can is either orange, lemon or strawberry flavour.
The ratio of the number of

**cans of orange : cans of lemon : cans of strawberry** is 4 : 5 : 1

$\frac{1}{3}$ of the orange flavour cans are fizzy.

30% of the lemon flavour cans are fizzy.

$\frac{1}{2}$ of the strawberry flavour cans are fizzy.

Work out the ratio of the number of **fizzy : not fizzy** drinks on the shelf.
Give your answer in its simplest form. **(5 marks)**

**D6.** There are two children's sports groups in a town.

In one group there are 48 children aged 10 and under and 60 children over 10.

In the other group, $\frac{4}{9}$ of the children are aged 10 and under and the rest are over 10.

Daniel says, 'The ratio of the number of children

**aged 10 and under : aged over 10**

is the same for both groups.'

Is Daniel correct?

You must show how you get your answer. **(3 marks)**

**D7.** Anne, Kemal and Charlie collect stamps.

The ratio number of stamps collected by

**Annie : Kemal : Charlie** is 9 : 11 : 15

Charlie has 24 more stamps than Annie.

How many stamps does Kemal have? **(3 marks)**

**D8.** Liam, Helen and Garry each earn the same monthly salary.

Liam spends 64% of his salary and saves the rest.

For Helen's salary, the ratio amount saved : amount spent is 2 : 3.

Garry spends $\frac{5}{8}$ of his salary and saves the rest.

Work out who saves the greatest percentage of their salary each month.

You must show how you get the answer. **(4 marks)**

You do not need to find the amount of money they actually save. You only need to find the percentage of their salary that each saves every month.

**D9.** There are some marbles in a bag.

$\frac{1}{4}$ of the marbles are purple. The rest of the marbles are yellow.

Write down the ratio

**number of purple marbles : number of yellow marbles**

Give your answer in the form 1 : $n$. **(2 marks)**

**D10.** The ratio of number of students studying A Level Maths : A Level Physics is 7 : 3

The ratio of number of students studying A Level Physics : A Level Politics is 5 : 6

There are 54 students studying A Level Politics.

Work out the number of students studying A Level Maths. **(4 marks)**

## Ratio and proportion Set E

**E1.** A box contains only red balloons, blue balloons and white balloons.

The ratio of the number of

**red balloons : blue balloons : yellow balloons** is 3 : 9 : 7

There are 16 fewer red balloons than yellow balloons.

Work out the total number of balloons in the box. **(3 marks)**

**E2.** The container in the diagram is $\frac{3}{4}$ full of water.

A jar holds 225 ml of water.

What is the greatest number of jars that can be completely filled with water from the container? **(4 marks)**

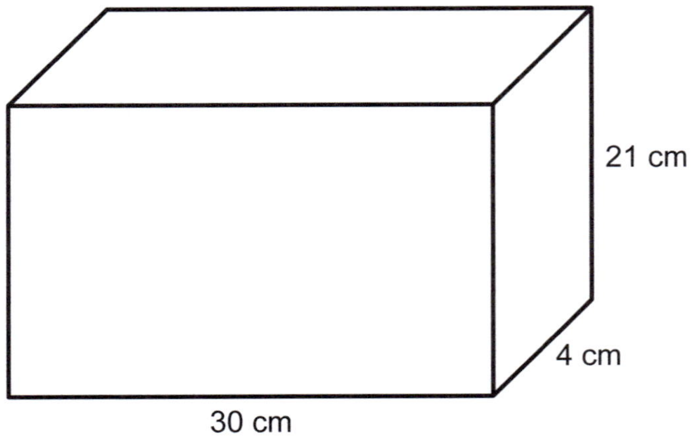


1 cm³ = 1 ml

volume of cuboid = width × length × height

**E3.** Kira is 5 years older than Mia.

Alba is twice as old as Kira.

The sum of their three ages is 95

Find the ratio of Kira's age to Mia's age to Alba's age.

Give your answer in its simplest form. **(4 marks)**

**E4.** In Deeville sports club, the ratio of the number of children to the number of adults is 3 : 2.

40% of children and $\frac{1}{4}$ of adults train every Saturday morning.

What percentage of all people in the sports club train every Saturday morning? **(4 marks)**

**E5.** In a company, 60% of employees are over 25 years old.

The ratio of employees who are

**under 25 who drive to work : under 25 who do not drive to work**

is 3 : 2.

Calculate the percentage of all employees that are under 25 and do not drive into work. **(4 marks)**

**E6.** In the Northern Hemisphere, $\frac{3}{5}$ of the total area is water.
In the Southern Hemisphere, the ratio **area of land : area of water** is 1 : 4
Work out the percentage of the earth's surface that is water. **(4 marks)**

**E7.** The points A, B and C are such that ABC is a straight line.
The coordinates of A are (−3, 3).
The coordinates of B are (6, 9).
AB : BC = 3 : 2
Find the coordinates of C. **(5 marks)**

**E8.** The points L, M and N are three points in a straight line.
LM : MN = 4 : 5
The coordinates of L are (−5, 2).
The coordinates of N are (13, 11).
Work out the coordinates of M. **(5 marks)**

**E9.** The length of an aeroplane is 23.4 metres.
Leon makes a scale model of the aeroplane.
The scale is 1 : 26
Work out the length of the model plane.
Give your answer in centimetres. **(3 marks)**

**E10.** Here is a plan of a garden drawn to a scale of 1 : 20

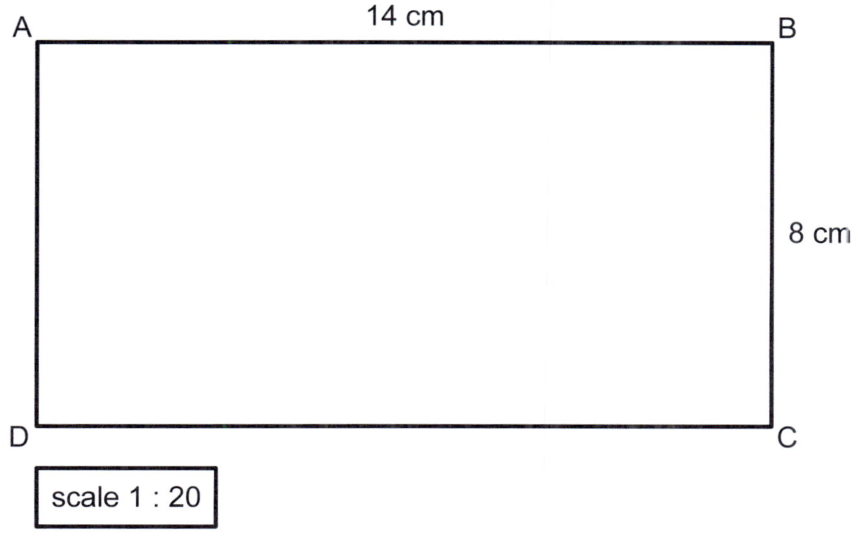


Work out the area of the actual garden.
Give your answer in square metres. **(3 marks)**

First, use the given scale to calculate the length and width of the actual garden. Then, multiply these to find the area of the actual garden.
Remember that 1 m = 100 cm.

# End of Chapter Notes

You could try and complete the 10 questions in each set, in a single study session. This may help with exam practice and keeping the focus going even when the questions are challenging.

| 1. |
| --- |
| 2. |
| 3. |

Write 3 things you feel you need to keep an eye on.

| 1. |
| --- |
| 2. |
| 3. |

Write 3 common mistakes that either you or your friends may make.

You could write specific mistakes or whole questions that you feel are easy to make a mistake on.

| 1. |
| --- |
| 2. |
| 3. |

**Well done for completing this chapter!**

# Chapter 3
# Money

*"You can not delegate learning. Only you can do it! Keep going!."*

**Worked Solutions**

# Money: Worked examples

**Here are four worked examples to get you started on this topic.**

- **Look at each example in turn.**
- **Can you do the question independently?**
- **If not, go over it slowly and work through the solution.**

### Worked example 1

Izzy invests £2500 in a savings account for 4 years.

The account pays simple interest at a rate of 2.5% per year.

**a)** Work out the total amount of interest Izzy gets by the end of the 4 years. **(3 marks)**

**b)** Work out the total amount Izzy receives after 4 years. **(2 marks)**

### Solution

| | |
|---|---|
| **a)** As a decimal, 2.5% = 0.025<br>£2500 × 0.025 = £62.50 **(1 mark)**<br>£62.50 × 4 **(1 mark)**<br>= £250 **(1 mark)** | Write 2.5% as a decimal.<br>Work out the amount of interest for 1 year.<br>Multiply the interest for 1 year by 4 as there are 4 years. |
| **b)** Total amount<br>= initial amount + interest earned<br>= £2500 + £250 **(1 mark)**<br>= £2750 **(1 mark)** | Remember to add the amount that she has to begin with to the interest she earns. |

### Worked example 2

Nishita invested £800 for 4 years in a savings account.

By the end of the 4 years she has received a total of £80 simple interest.

Work out the annual rate of simple interest. **(3 marks)**

### Solution

| | |
|---|---|
| The amount of interest per year<br>= £80 ÷ 4 = £20 **(1 mark)** | For simple interest, divide the total amount of interest by the number of years to find the amount of interest earned each year. |
| interest rate = $\frac{20}{800} \times 100\%$ **(1 mark)**<br>= 2.5% **(1 mark)** | interest rate<br>$= \frac{\text{amount of interest earned in 1 year}}{\text{amount of money invested}} \times 100\%$ |

### Worked example 3

Jake invests £3200 in a savings account for 4 years.
The account pays compound interest at a rate of 2.1% per year.
Work out the total amount of interest Jake gets by the end of the 4 years. **(4 marks)**

### Solution

**Step 1:** find the multiplier
100% + 2.1% = 102.1% = 1.021
**(1 mark)**

When you enter 102.1% in to a calculator, then press equals, the calculator changes the answer to a fraction or decimal.
If you are unsure, learn how to use your calculator.

**Step 2:** use the formula
total amount in the bank after 4 years
= £3200 × $(1.021)^4$ **(1 mark)**
= £3477.39 **(1 mark)**

Learn this formula!
total amount after $n$ years
= starting amount × $(\text{multiplier})^n$

**Step 3:** calculate the interest earned
interest = £3477.39 − £3200
= £277.39 **(1 mark)**

interest earned
= final amount − starting amount

For all money questions, you should only give your final answer to 2 decimal places – you can't have anything smaller than 1p.

## Worked example 4

Stuart invests £2800 in a savings account for 4 years.

The account pays compound interest at a rate of 1% for the first year and 0.8% for every year after the first year.

How much money will there be at the bank at the end of Year 4? **(5 marks)**

## Solution

| | |
|---|---|
| The multiplier for the first year<br>= 100% + 1% = 101% = 1.01 **(1 mark)**<br>The multiplier for the years 2, 3 and 4<br>= 100% + 0.8% = 100.8% = 1.008 **(1 mark)** | If there is different interest for each year, calculate the multipliers separately. |
| Total amount at the end of 4 years<br>= £2800 × 1.01 × $1.008^3$ **(1 mark)**<br>= £2896.42 (2 d.p) **(1 mark)** | Multiply £2800 by 1.01 to find the amount at the end of the first year, then by $1.008^3$ to find the amount at the end of the 4th year. |
| Interest earned<br>= £2896.42 − £2800 = £96.42 **(1 mark)** | Remember that interest earned = final amount − initial amount |

Now try each set of questions.

You might want to create a table like this in your exercise book to record your progress.

You could try and complete the 10 questions in each set, in a single study session.

This may help with exam practice and keeping the focus going even when the questions are challenging.

| Study session | Question set | Tick when completed | How do I feel about these questions? Difficult – I need to improve my understanding of ... |
|---|---|---|---|
| 1 | A | | |
| 2 | B | | |
| 3 | C | | |
| 4 | D | | |
| 5 | E | | |

Remember, there is no ‘quick fix’ when problem solving. If you are stuck, this is a good thing. It means you are being challenged and you are learning.

Worked Solutions are here **https://www.oliviapresspublishers.com**

**All diagrams** in this chapter are not drawn accurately unless otherwise stated.

**GCSE students** can use a calculator unless they see this symbol 

**International GCSE students** can use a calculator in all the questions.

## Money Set A

**A1.** Maria invests £4500 in a savings account for 3 years.
The account pays simple interest at a rate of 1.8% per year.
Work out the total amount of interest Maria gets by the end of the 3 years. **(3 marks)**

**A2.** Abdul invests £200 000 in a savings account for 2 years.
The account pays compound interest at a rate of 1.5 % per annum.
Calculate the total amount of interest Abdul will get at the end of 2 years. **(3 marks)**

**A3.** Ruby wants to invest £40 000 for 3 years in a bank.

| **Bank X** | **Bank Y** |
|---|---|
| Compound interest | Simple interest |
| 2% for each year | 2% for each year |

Which bank will give Ruby the most interest at the end of 3 years?
You must show all your working. **(4 marks)**

Find the interest for each bank then compare the amounts.

**A4.** Northern Bank has two types of account.
Both accounts pay compound interest.

| **Cash savings account** | **Shares account** |
|---|---|
| Interest | Interest |
| 2.5% per annum | 3.5% per annum |

Ali invests £3000 in the cash savings account.
Ben invests £2600 in the shares account.

**a)** Work out who will get the most interest by the end of 3 years.
You must show all your working. **(5 marks)**

In the third year the rate of interest for the shares account is changed to 4% per annum.

**b)** Does this affect who will get the most interest by the end of 3 years?
Give a reason for your answer. **(1 mark)**

**A5.** Remi invests £900 for 5 years in a savings account.
By the end of the 5 years he has received a total of £135 simple interest.
Work out the annual rate of simple interest. **(3 marks)**

**A6.** Anil wants to invest £40 000 for 3 years in a savings account.

| **Bank X** | **Bank Y** |
|---|---|
| Compound interest | Compound interest |
| 2.2% for each year | 2% for the first year and an additional 0.9% for extra years |

Which bank will give Anil the most interest at the end of 3 years?
You must show all your working **(5 marks)**

**A7.** Amy is planning a trip to a theme park for one adult and three children.
These are the costs for the trip.

| | |
|---|---|
| total cost of petrol | £36 |
| tickets to theme park | £28 for each adult |
| | £17.50 for each child |
| food | £20 for each adult |
| | £10 for each child |

Amy has £160.
How much more money does she need to pay for the trip? **(4 marks)**

**A8.** A shop sells jars of cookies.
Each jar costs £3.50.
Tahlia has £24.

**a)** Work out the greatest number of jars Tahlia can buy. **(2 marks)**

In a sale the jars are sold at half price.

Tahlia thinks she can buy exactly twice the number of jars for £24.

**b)** Is Tahlia correct? You must give a reason for your answer. **(2 marks)**

**A9.** Jordan buys seven notebooks.
He pays with £30 note and gets four 50p coins change.
How much does one notebook cost? **(3 marks)**

**A10.** Xav buys some birthday cards.
Each card costs £1.50.
He pays with a £20 note and gets £11 change.
Work out the number of birthday cards Xav buys. **(3 marks)**

To change a fraction to percentage, multiply the fraction by 100.

## Money Set B

**B1.** At the end of November, Nabeel's electricity meter reads 76 238 kWh.

At the end of December, the meter reads 77 938 kWh.

Each kWh of electricity Nabeel uses costs 25p.

Work out how much Nabeel had to pay for the electricity he used in December.

Give your answer in pounds. **(4 marks)**

**B2.** Maisie buys:

- 1 loaf of bread for £2.30
- 1 bottle of milk for £1.20
- 2 boxes of cereal for £2.80

She pays with £10 note.

She says, 'I should get £1.90 change.'

Is Maisie correct?

You must show how you got your answer. **(4 marks)**

**B3.** 3 kg of carrots cost £2.40

2 kg of carrots and 6 bags of apples cost £13.60

Work out the total cost of 5 kg of carrots and 2 bags of apples. **(4 marks)**

**B4.** Lorcan buys a bike for £80.

He sells it for £64.

Work out the percentage loss. **(3 marks)**

$$\text{percentage loss} = \frac{\text{loss}}{\text{original amount}} \times 100\%$$

**B5.** Amber pays £10 for 28 cupcakes.

She eats 2 cupcakes and sells the rest for 50p each.

Work out Amber's percentage profit. **(3 marks)**

$$\text{percentage profit} = \frac{\text{profit}}{\text{original amount}} \times 100\%$$

**B6.** At the end of 2023:

- the value of a house in the city centre was £280 000
- the value of the house in the village nearby was £210 000.

At the end of 2024:

- the value of a house in the city centre had decreased by 20%
- the value of the house in the village nearby had increased by 15%.

Which house had the greater value at the end of 2024? **(5 marks)**

**B7.** In a shop, a laptop has a normal price of £800.
The shop has a sale with 20% off all prices.
Lucas get a 10% student discount on all the items, including the sale items.
The 10% student discount is applied *after* the 20% reduction is applied.
Lucas has £560 to spend.
Does Lucas have enough money to buy the laptop? **(4 marks)**

**B8.** Evie is on a school trip in the USA.
She wants to buy a pair of trainers.
The trainers cost $70 in USA.
The same trainers cost £60 in UK. The exchange rate is $1 = £0.789
Use a suitable approximation to show that it is best to buy the trainers in USA. **(2 marks)**

**B9.** Rehan has saved £200 to buy some new clothes. He buys:

- three tops costing £15 each
- one pair of trainers costing £42
- two pair of jeans costing £35 each.

He also wants to buy a winter jacket costing £80.
Does he have enough money?
You must show how you got the answer. **(3 marks)**

**B10.** Jasmine is planning a holiday for four people for a week.
Here are the costs for the holiday for **each person**.

| travel: £250<br>hotel: £80 for each day<br>spending money: £300 |
|---|

Work out the total cost of the holiday for 4 people for 7 days. **(4 marks)**

## Money Set C

**C1.** Mo pays £12 for 30 highlighters.
Mo sells the highlighters for 50p each.
Work out Mo's percentage profit. **(3 marks)**

$$\text{percentage profit} = \frac{\text{profit}}{\text{original amount}} \times 100\%$$

**C2.** Two local shops sell boxes of the same type of breakfast cereal.
Each shop has a special offer.

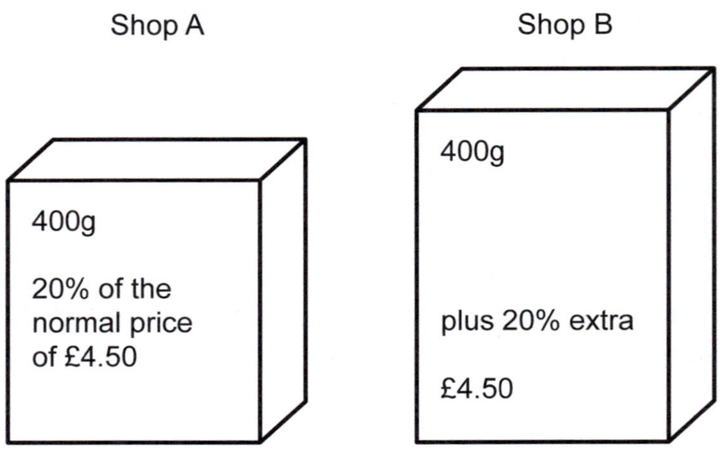


Which shop has the box of cereal that is the better value for money?
You must show your working. **(5 marks)**

**C3.** At the end of the year, a bonus of £3600 is shared by eight people who work for a delivery company.

40% of the bonus is shared equally between three managers.

The rest of the bonus is shared equally between five drivers.

One of the managers says, 'If the bonus was shared equally between all the people that work in the company, I would get 20% less money.'

Is the manager correct?
You must show how you get your answer. **(5 marks)**

**C4.** A unit of gas costs 6.2 pence.
On average Matilda uses 80.1 units of gas a week.
She pays for the gas she uses in 11 weeks.

**a)** Work out an estimate for the amount Matilda pays. **(2 marks)**

**b)** Is your answer an underestimate or an overestimate?
Explain your answer. **(2 marks)**

**C5.** One lollipop costs 35p.
Nikita buys eight lollipops and she has 44p left.

**a)** How much money does Nikita have in total?
Give your answer in pounds and pence. **(2 marks)**

If Nikita buys six lollipops, she has exactly the right amount of money left over to buy three sweets.

**b)** Work out the price of one sweet. **(2 marks)**

**C6.** In the school canteen, three cakes and two orange juices cost £3.25
Two cakes and three orange juices cost £3.55
Cian buys five cakes and five orange juices.

**a)** Work out how much Cian pays. **(2 marks)**

Elodie buys one cake and one orange juice.

**b)** Work out the price of one cake and one orange juice. **(2 marks)**

**C7.** Maya delivers newspapers 6 days a week.
The delivery takes 55 minutes each day.

**a)** Work out the number of hours and minutes that Maya takes in total. **(2 marks)**

Maya is paid £6.20 per hour.

**b)** Work out the amount of money Maya earns in one week. **(2 marks)**

**C8.** Aisha is buying cupcakes for a party.
She needs 30 cupcakes. She wants to choose one of these deals.

| **Deal A** | **Deal B** | **Deal C** |
|---|---|---|
| a box of 5<br>£5.49 per box<br>3 boxes for the price of 2. | a box of 10 for £8.50 | single cupcakes<br>90p each |

Which deal should Aisha choose? **(5 marks)**

**C9.** Tom buys 300 pens at 15p each.
He wants to make 40% profit on each of the pens.

**a)** What should the selling price of a pen be? **(2 marks)**

**b)** How much will Tom's total sales be?
Give your answer in pounds. **(2 marks)**

**C10.** 30% of a number is 21
What is 70% of the number? **(3 marks)**

## Money Set D

**D1.** A jumper is reduced by 40%.
The sale price is £36
What was the original price? **(3 marks)**

You could either use a multiplier or work out what percentage of the original price £36 is.

**D2.** The prices of all bags are reduced by 20% in a sale.
The sale price of a bag is £48
What was the original price? **(3 marks)**

**D3.** Olly is buying lightbulbs for a new office building.
He needs 60 lightbulbs.

| **Deal A** | **Deal B** | **Deal C** |
|---|---|---|
| a pack of 4 lightbulbs for £7.50<br>buy 3 packs for the price of 2 packs | a box of 10 lightbulbs for £11.99 | single bulbs<br>£1.99 each |

Which deal should Olly choose? **(5 marks)**

**D4.** Milk is sold in three different size cartons.

| **Option 1** | **Option 2** | **Option 3** |
|---|---|---|
| 2.2 litres for £1.74 | 1.2 litres for £0.95 | 500 ml for 45p |

**a)** Which option is the cheapest? **(2 marks)**
**b)** Which option is the most expensive? **(1 mark)**

**D5.** In a sale, the normal price of a notebook is reduced by 30%.
The sale price of the notebook is £3.50
Work out the normal price of the notebook. **(3 marks)**

**D6.** Emily buys a pack of 24 bottles of water.
The pack costs £8.40
Emily drinks one bottle of water herself. She sells the rest for 65p each.
Work out Emily's percentage profit.
Give your answer correct to 2 significant figures. **(4 marks)**

**D7.** Raya buys a van for £8500 plus VAT at 20%.

Raya pays a deposit for the van.

She then pays the rest of the cost in 12 equal payments of £531.25 each month.

Find the ratio of the deposit to the total payment.

Give your answer in its simplest form. **(5 marks)**

**D8.** Fleur buys a house for £246 500

She sells the house for £258 220

Calculate the percentage profit Fleur makes.

Give your answer to 2 decimal places. **(3 marks)**

$$\text{percentage profit} = \frac{\text{actual profit}}{\text{original amount}} \times 100\%$$

**D9.** Eva wants to buy 38 T-shirts for the people in the school choir.

Each T-shirt costs £5.90.

Eva does the calculation 40 × 6 = 240 to estimate the cost of 38 T-shirts.

**a)** Explain how Eva's calculation shows the actual cost will be less than £240 **(1 mark)**

There is an offer on the T-shirts.

| T-shirts £5.90 each. |
|---|
| Buy 20 or more T-shirts. |
| Get 12% off the total cost. |

**b)** Work out the actual cost of buying 38 T-shirts using the special offer **(4 marks)**

**D10.** Mihailo buys a boat.

The cost of the boat is £17 200 plus VAT at 20%.

Mihailo pays a deposit of £5000

He pays the rest of the cost in 10 equal payments.

Work out the amount of each of the 10 payments. **(4 marks)**

## Money Set E

**E1.** Archie changes £950 into South African rand.

He wants to get as many 500 rand notes as possible.

The exchange rate is £1 = 22.92 rand.

Work out the greatest number of 500 rand notes that Archie can get for £950 **(3 marks)**

**E2.** Selim went on holiday to Bermuda.

His flights cost a total of £1600.

Selim stayed for 12 nights.

His hotel room cost $215 per night.

Selim hired a car to use on the island.

The cost of renting a car was $25 per day.

He hired the car for 9 days.

The exchange rate was $1.20 = £1.

Work out the total cost of the flights, the hotel room and the car.

Give your answer in pounds. **(5 marks)**

**E3.** Milic works in a restaurant. Here are her rates of pay:

| Day | Rate of pay |
|---|---|
| Monday to Friday | £8.40 per hour |
| Weekend | £11.20 per hour |

Milic worked for a total of 20 hours last week.

She worked 40% of these 20 hours at the weekend.

Show that Milic was paid less than £200 last week. **(4 marks)**

**E4.** Emma gets a bonus of 35% of her monthly pay.

She is paid £2800 per month.

Nick gets a bonus of 40% of his monthly pay.

He is paid £1700

Work out the difference between the bonus Emma gets and the bonus Nick gets. **(3 marks)**

**E5.** Paru wants to buy a washing machine.

The washing machine costs £592

Paru will pay a deposit of £120

She will then pay the rest of the cost in 4 equal monthly payments.

How much is each monthly payment? **(4 marks)**

**E6.** There are 18 rows of seats in a theatre.
There are 15 seats in each row.
A play was shown in the theatre on Saturday.
80% of the seats were sold.
The tickets that were sold cost a total of £2052
How much does a ticket cost? **(3 marks)**

**E7.** Last year the cost of a season ticket for a football club was £560
This year the cost of a season ticket for the club has increased to £644
Work out the percentage increase in the cost of a season ticket. **(2 marks)**

$$\text{percentage increase} = \frac{\text{actual increase}}{\text{original value}} \times 100\%$$

**E8.** Mr Lewis uses oil to heat his home.
The oil is kept in a tank.
At the beginning of November, Mr Lewis bought enough oil to fill the tank completely.
He paid 65p per litre for this oil.
He paid a total amount of £975.
At the end of February Mr Lewis had 450 litres of oil in the tank.
He bought enough oil to fill the tank completely.
The cost of oil had increased by 20%.
Work out the total amount Mr Lewis paid for the oil he bought in February. **(5 marks)**

**E9.** Here are the charges at a car park in Spain.
Juan parked his car in this car park.
Juan drove into the car park at 10.35 am.

| **Car park charges (euros, €)** |
|---|
| 85 cents per 10 minutes |

When he drove out of the car park he had to pay €7.65
At what time did Juan drive out of the car park? **(3 marks)**

**E10.** Silva works in a restaurant. Here are her rates of pay.

| Day | Rate of pay |
|---|---|
| Weekday | £6.50 per hour |
| Weekend | £$x$ per hour |

She worked 20 hours at the weekend.
She was paid £250 last week.
The ratio of the weekday hours : weekend hours = 4 : 5
Work out the value of $x$. **(4 marks)**

# End of Chapter Notes

You could try and complete the 10 questions in each set, in a single study session. This may help with exam practice and keeping the focus going even when the questions are challenging.

| 1. |
|---|
| 2. |
| 3. |

Write 3 things you feel you need to keep an eye on.

| 1. |
|---|
| 2. |
| 3. |

Write 3 common mistakes that either you or your friends may make.

You could write specific mistakes or whole questions that you feel are easy to make a mistake on.

| 1. |
|---|
| 2. |
| 3. |

## Well done for completing this chapter!

# Chapter 4
# Data

*"If you don't like the road you are walking, start paving a new one." – Dolly Parton*

**Worked Solutions**

# Data: Worked examples

**Here are seven worked examples to get you started on this topic.**

- **Look at each example in turn.**
- **Can you do the question independently?**
- **If not, go over it slowly and work through the solution.**

## Worked example 1

There are 30 children in class 11A.

7 children play basketball.

12 children play football.

6 children play both basketball and football.

Find the number of children that do not play basketball or football. **(4 marks)**

In this question, there is one variable (basketball/football), so you can draw a Venn diagram.

## Solution

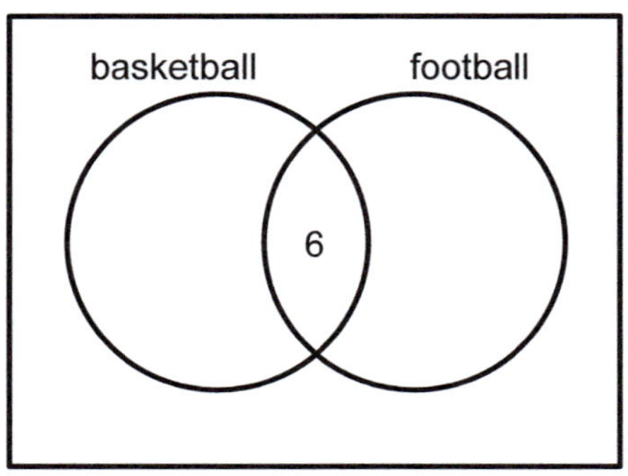


Draw a Venn diagram.
6 children play both basketball and football, so write 6 in the intersection.

**(1 mark)**

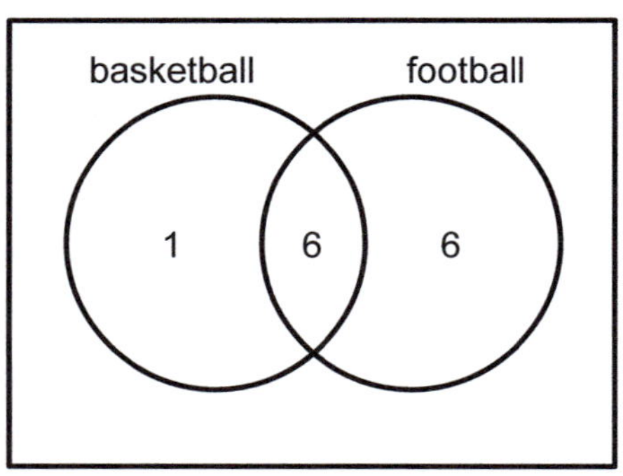


7 children play basketball.

7 − 6 = 1 child plays only basketball. **(1 mark)**

12 children play football.

So 12 − 6 = 6 children play only football. **(1 mark)**

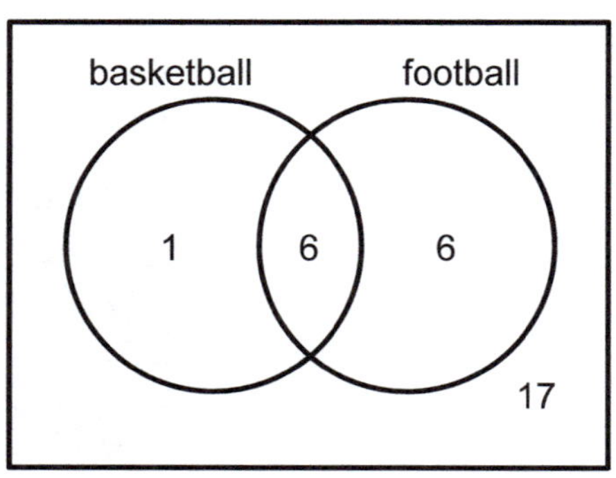


30 children in the class.

30 – 1 – 6 – 6 = 17 do not play basketball or football. **(1 mark)**

### Worked example 2

There are 28 children in class 10C.
18 children cycle to school.
15 children are girls.
7 of the girls cycle to school.

**a)** Find the number of boys that do not cycle to school. **(3 marks)**

A child is chosen at random from class 10C.

**b)** Write down the probability that the child is a boy that cycles to school. **(2 marks)**

Because there are two variables (boy/girl AND cycle/not cycle), you will need to draw a two-way table to answer this question.

### Solution

**a)**

| | **Boys** | **Girls** | **Total** |
|---|---|---|---|
| **Cycle** | | 7 | **18** |
| **Not cycle** | | | |
| **Total** | | **15** | **28** |

Draw a two-way table and write in the information you are given.

| | **Boys** | **Girls** | **Total** |
|---|---|---|---|
| **Cycle** | 11 | 7 | **18** |
| **Not cycle** | 2 | 8 | **10** |
| **Total** | **13** | **15** | **28** |

2 children are boys that do not cycle to school.

18 − 7 = 11 boys cycle to school
15 − 7 = 8 girls do not cycle to school **(1 mark for two correct)**
28 − 18 = 10 children do not cycle
28 − 15 = 13 children are boys **(1 mark for two correct)**
10 − 8 = 2 children are boys that do not cycle to school **(1 mark)**

**b)** P(boy that cycles) = $\frac{11}{28}$ **(1 mark)**

There are 28 children in total.
11 of these are boys that cycle to school.

## Worked example 3

There are 8 cubes in a bowl.

7 of the cubes are purple and 1 is yellow.

The mean mass of all the 8 cubes is 156 g.

The mean mass of the purple cubes is 150 g.

Work out the mass of the yellow cube. **(3 marks)**

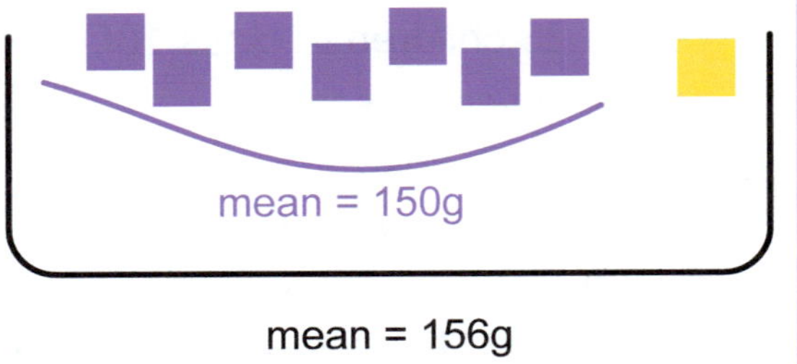


## Solution

| | |
|---|---|
| $156\text{ g} = \dfrac{\text{total mass of all cubes}}{8}$<br>total mass of all cubes = 156 g × 8<br>= 1248 g **(1 mark)** | Using:<br>mean mass of all 8 cubes<br>$= \dfrac{\text{total mass of all cubes}}{8}$ |
| $150\text{ g} = \dfrac{\text{total mass of purple cubes}}{7}$<br>total mass of purple cubes = 150 g × 7<br>= 1050 g<br>**(1 mark)** | Using:<br>mean mass of purple cubes<br>$= \dfrac{\text{total mass of purple cubes}}{\text{number of purple cubes}}$ |
| mass of yellow cube = 1248 g − 1050 g<br>= 198 g **(1 mark)** | Using:<br>mass of yellow cube<br>= total mass of all cubes − total mass of purple cubes |

### Worked example 4

The table shows some information about the mass of 50 shells.

| Mass, $w$ (g) | Frequency |
|---|---|
| $0 < w \leqslant 20$ | 12 |
| $20 < w \leqslant 30$ | 14 |
| $30 < w \leqslant 40$ | 13 |
| $40 < w \leqslant 50$ | 6 |
| $50 < w \leqslant 60$ | 5 |

Work out the mean mass of the shells. **(4 marks)**

### Solution

| Mass, $w$ (g) | Frequency | Midpoint | Midpoint × frequency |
|---|---|---|---|
| $0 < w \leqslant 20$ | 12 | 10 | 10 × 12 = 120 |
| $20 < w \leqslant 30$ | 14 | 25 | 25 × 14 = 350 |
| $30 < w \leqslant 40$ | 13 | 35 | 35 × 13 = 455 |
| $40 < w \leqslant 50$ | 6 | 45 | 45 × 6 = 270 |
| $50 < w \leqslant 60$ | 5 | 55 | 55 × 5 = 275 |
| **Total** | **50** | | **1470** |

**(1 mark for correct midpoints)**
**(1 mark for correct multiplication midpoint × frequency)**

1. Add two extra columns to the table.
2. Find the midpoint of each interval.
3. Multiply it by the frequency.
4. Add all the results.
5. Add all the frequency values.

mean $= \frac{1470}{50}$ **(1 mark)**

$= 29.4$ g **(1 mark)**

mean $= \frac{\text{sum of (midpoint × frequency)}}{\text{total frequency}}$

## Worked example 5

There was a total of 120 students from Year 10 and 11 at a sports day.

75 students were from Year 11.

29 of the Year 10 students were in the 800 m running race.

46 students took part in the 800 m running race.

**a)** Copy and complete the frequency tree. **(3 marks)**

One of the 120 students is chosen at random.

**b)** Work out the probability that the student is from Year 11 and did not take part in the 800 m running race. **(1 mark)**

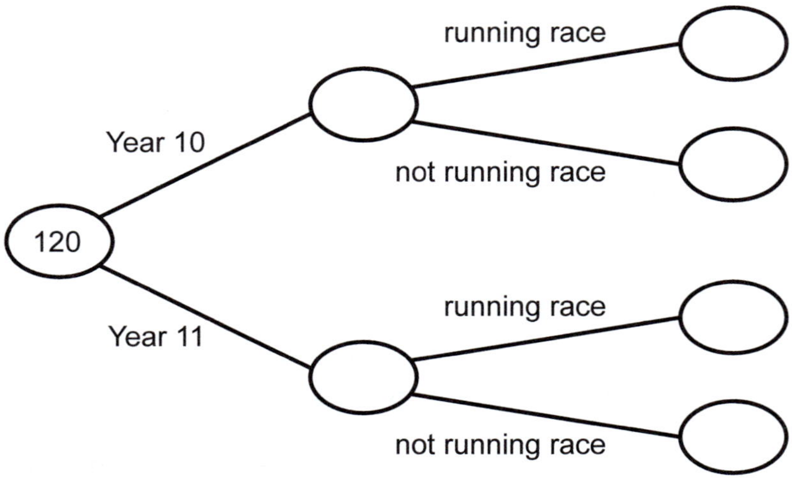


## Solution

**a)**

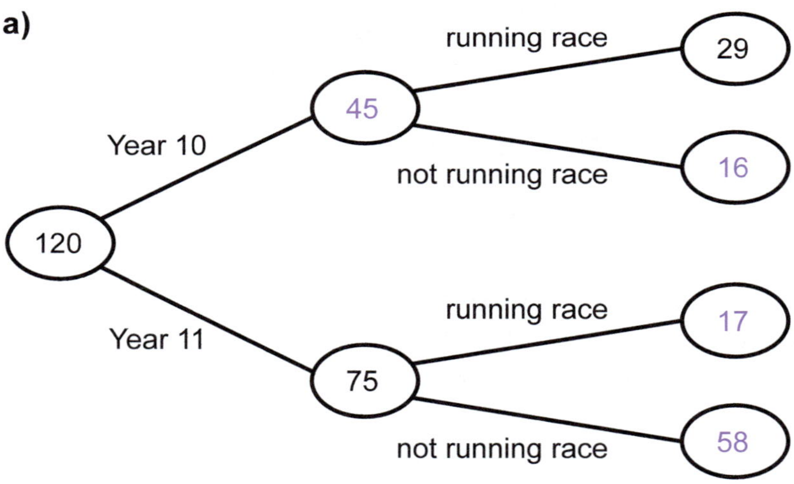


**(1 mark for completing the frequency tree)**

number of Year 10 students = 120 − 75 = 45

number of Year 10 students not running = 45 − 29 = 16

**(1 mark for 2 correct answers)**

number of Year 11 students running = 46 − 29 = 17

number of Year 11 students not running = 75 − 17 = 58

**(1 mark for 2 correct answers)**

**b)** probability of Year 11 student not running = $\frac{58}{120} = \frac{29}{60}$

**(1 mark)**

Give your answer in its simplest form.

### Worked example 6

There are red, purple, yellow and blue cubes in a box.
The table shows the probability of picking a red cube from the box.

| **Colour** | red | purple | yellow | blue |
|---|---|---|---|---|
| **Probability** | 0.28 | | | |

number of purple cubes = number of yellow cubes = number of blue cubes

**a)** Copy and complete the probability table. **(2 marks)**

There are 14 red cubes.

**b)** Work out the total number of cubes in the box. **(2 marks)**

### Solution

**a)** probability of not red
= 1 − 0.28 = 0.72 **(1 mark)**

P(purple) = P(yellow) = P(blue)
= 0.72 ÷ 3
= 0.24 **(1 mark)**

| **Colour** | red | purple | yellow | blue |
|---|---|---|---|---|
| **Probability** | 0.28 | 0.24 | 0.24 | 0.24 |

Remember that probabilities always add up to 1.

Since there are the same number of purple, yellow and blue cubes, the probability of each of these is the same.

**b)**

| | *% of all cubes* | *Number of cubes* | |
|---|---|---|---|
| | 28% | 14 cubes | |
| ÷14 | 2% | 1 cube | ÷14 |
| ×50 | 100% | 50 cubes | ×50 |

**(1 mark)**

There are 50 cubes in the box **(1 mark)**

Use the fact that 0.28 = 28%

## Worked example 7

The probability tree diagram shows the probabilities of Matilda winning two quizzes, one on films and the other on music.

**a)** Copy and complete the tree diagram. **(2 marks)**

film quiz music quiz

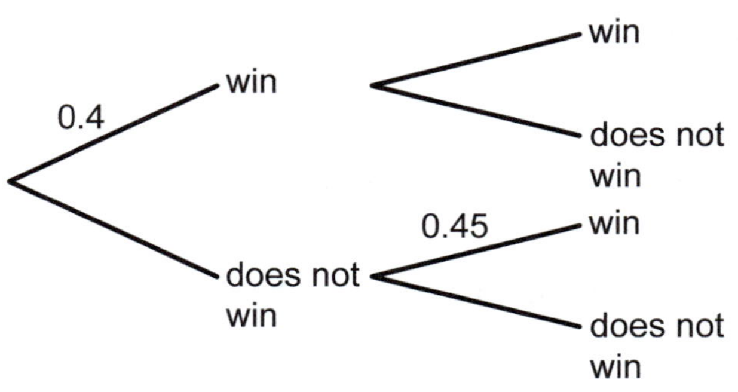


**b)** Work out the probability that Matilda wins only one of the quizzes. **(3 marks)**

## Solution

**a)** film quiz music quiz

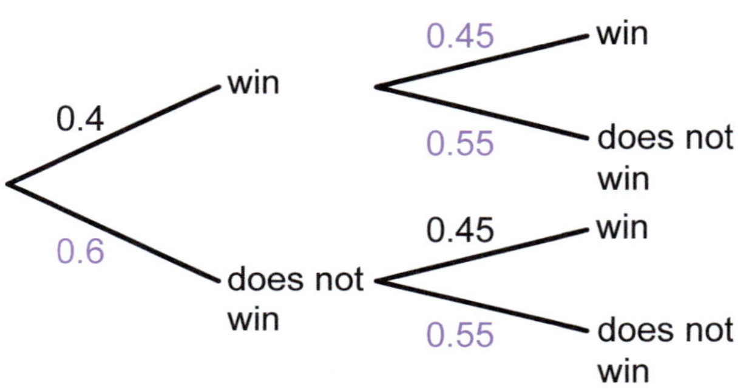


The probability in every branch of the tree adds up to 1.

P(does not win film quiz) $= 1 - 0.4 = 0.6$

P(does not win music quiz) $= 1 - 0.45 = 0.55$

**b)** probability of winning the film quiz and not winning the music quiz $= 0.4 \times 0.55 = 0.22$ **(1 mark)**

probability of not winning the film quiz and winning the music quiz $= 0.6 \times 0.45 = 0.27$ **(1 mark)**

probability of winning one quiz only $= 0.22 + 0.27 = 0.49$ **(1 mark)**

When you go along the branches, multiply the probabilities.

film quiz music quiz

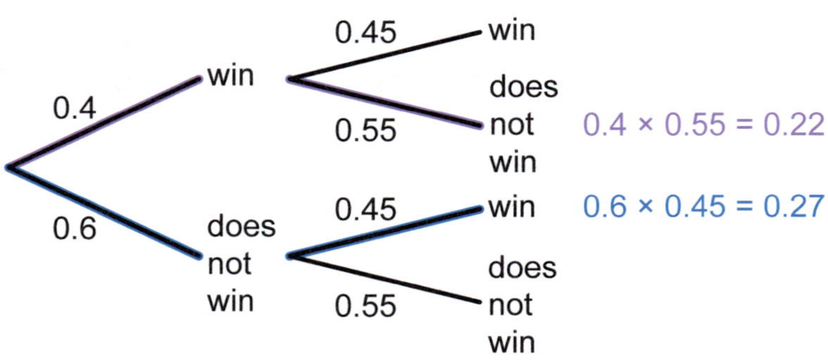


When you want to find the probability of two different routes through the tree, add the probability of each route.

Now try each set of questions.

You might want to create a table like this in your exercise book to record your progress.

You could try and complete the 10 questions in each set, in a single study session.

This may help with exam practice and keeping the focus going even when the questions are challenging.

| **Study session** | **Question set** | **Tick when completed** | **How do I feel about these questions? Difficult – I need to improve my understanding of …** |
|---|---|---|---|
| 1 | A | | |
| 2 | B | | |
| 3 | C | | |
| 4 | D | | |
| 5 | E | | |

Remember, there is no 'quick fix' when problem solving. If you are stuck, this is a good thing. It means you are being challenged and you are learning.

Worked Solutions are here **https://www.oliviapresspublishers.com**

**All diagrams** in this chapter are not drawn accurately unless otherwise stated.

**GCSE students** can use a calculator unless they see this symbol 

**International GCSE students** can use a calculator in all the questions.

## Data Set A

**A1.** There are 30 children in class 11B.
8 of them are wearing a watch.
13 of them are wearing glasses.
5 of them are wearing both glasses and a watch.
How many of them are wearing neither glasses nor a watch? **(3 marks)**

Draw a Venn diagram similar to this one.

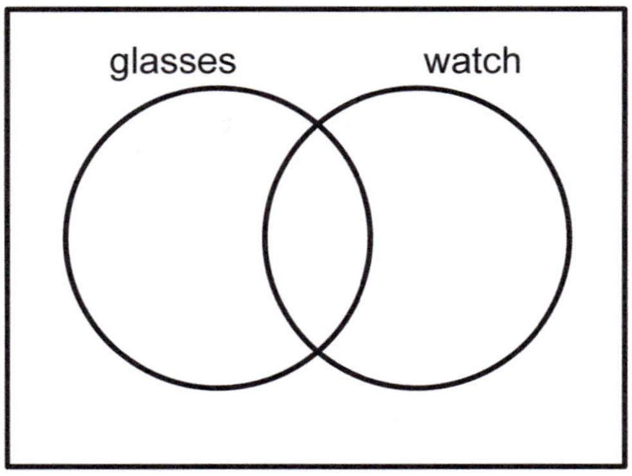


**A2.** There are 31 children in the school choir.
Out of the 31 children, 20 play an instrument and 15 sing.
Eight children both sing and play an instrument.
Work out the number of children who do not sing and do not play an instrument. **(4 marks)**

Draw a Venn diagram.

**A3.** There are 29 marbles in a jar.
Seven marbles are purple; the rest are blue.
13 of the marbles are in the shape of a cube. The rest are spheres.
Eight marbles are blue and in the shape of a cube.
A marble is chosen at random.
Work out the probability of the marble being blue and in the shape of a sphere. **(5 marks)**

Copy and complete the table.
How many marbles are there in total?
How many blue marbles in the shape of a sphere are there?

| | **Purple** | **Blue** | **Total** |
|---|---|---|---|
| **Cube** | | | |
| **Sphere** | | | |
| **Total** | | | |

**A4.** There are 30 children in class 11D.
20 children have school lunch.
18 of the children are girls.
12 of the girls have school lunch.

**a)** How many boys do not have school lunch? **(3 marks)**

**b)** A child is chosen at random.
Write down the probability that the child is a boy that has school lunch. **(2 marks)**

> Draw a two-way table.

**A5.** Here are the ages of eight children at a party.

5, 5, 9, 7, 7, 7, 8, 8

**a)** Write down the mode. **(1 mark)**

**b)** Work out the mean age of the children. **(1 mark)**

**c)** Work out the range of the ages of the children. **(1 mark)**

Another child comes to the party. This child is 7 years old.

**d)** Fleur thinks that the mean will not change.
Is Fleur correct? Explain why. **(2 marks)**

**A6.** Toby has five cards. Each card has a number on it.
The median of the cards is 9
The mode is 7
The range is 10
The mean is 10
What are the numbers on the cards? **(4 marks)**

> Suppose the 5 cards are arranged in ascending order from left to right. Since the median is 9, what is the number on the middle card?

**A7.** Matthew has five cards.
Each card has a number on it.
The median of the cards is 6
The mode is 7
The range is 5
The mean is 5
What could the cards be? **(4 marks)**

**A8.** Here is the number of goals scored by a football team in each of its first 10 games.

3, 2, 4, 2, 0, 2, 1, 0, 3, 1

**a)** Write down the mode. **(1 mark)**

**b)** Work out the mean number of goals for the first 10 games. **(2 marks)**

**c)** Work out the median number of goals. **(1 mark)**

**d)** In the 11th and 12th games, the team scored the same number of goals.

The mean number of goals for all 12 games is 2.

How many goals did the team score in each of the 11th and 12th games? **(3 marks)**

**A9.** The table shows the amount of pocket money some children from class 8A are given each week.

| Amount of pocket money (£) | Number of children |
| --- | --- |
| 0 | 2 |
| 1 | 7 |
| 2 | 8 |
| 3 | 4 |
| 4 | 2 |
| 5 | 1 |
| 6 | 3 |

**a)** How many children are there in class 8A? **(2 marks)**

**b)** What is the range of the pocket money in the class? **(1 mark)**

**c)** What is the mode? **(1 mark)**

**d)** What is the mean?
Give your answer to the nearest pound. **(2 marks)**

**A10.** The table shows some information about the number of miles Stuart ran in the last 30 days.

| Distance, $d$ (miles) | Number of days |
|---|---|
| $0 < d \leqslant 4$ | 7 |
| $4 < d \leqslant 8$ | 9 |
| $8 < d \leqslant 12$ | 8 |
| $12 < d \leqslant 16$ | 6 |

Stuart calculates the mean average distance he ran.
Here is Stuart's working:

| Distance, $d$ (miles) | Number of days | Midpoint |
|---|---|---|
| $0 < d \leqslant 4$ | 7 | 2 |
| $4 < d \leqslant 8$ | 9 | 6 |
| $8 < d \leqslant 12$ | 8 | 10 |
| $12 < d \leqslant 16$ | 6 | 14 |

total = 2 + 6 + 10 + 14 = 32 miles
mean = 32 ÷ 4 = 8 miles.

**a)** Give two reasons why Stuart is not correct. **(2 marks)**

**b)** Calculate the mean average distance that Stuart ran.
Give your answer correct to two decimal places. **(2 marks)**

## Data Set B

**B1.** There are 15 fish in an aquarium.
Seven fish are golden fish.
10 fish have stripes.
Two fish are not golden and do not have stripes.
How many fish are golden and do not have stripes?
**(3 marks)**

Draw a Venn diagram.

**B2.** Valma asks a group of children whether they speak Spanish or Italian.
Four children speak both Spanish and Italian.
21 children speak Italian.
13 children speak Spanish.
Two children do not speak Italian or Spanish.
How many children did Valma ask?
**(3 marks)**

Draw a Venn diagram.

**B3.** Becky sells home-made strawberry jam in jars.
The table shows her sales for the first 5 weeks.

| Week | Number of jars sold |
|---|---|
| 1 | 17 |
| 2 | 38 |
| 3 | 25 |
| 4 | 20 |
| 5 | $x$ |

The mean number of jars sold in the first 5 weeks was 28 jars.
Work out how many jars were sold in week 5. **(3 marks)**

**B4.** Carol keeps a record of the number of cars parked in the car park during the first week of May.

She works out that the mean number of cars in the car park is 52.

Here are her results for six of the days.

| Monday | Tuesday | Wednesday | Thursday | Friday | Saturday | Sunday |
|---|---|---|---|---|---|---|
| | 51 | 49 | 48 | 55 | 60 | 58 |

**a)** How many cars were there in the car park on Monday? **(3 marks)**

A car was chosen at random.

**b)** Work out the probability that it was parked at the weekend.
Give your answer as a fraction in simplified form. **(3 marks)**

**B5.** The table shows the distance Jo walks each day.

| **Day** | **Distance (km)** |
|---|---|
| Monday | 4 |
| Tuesday | |
| Wednesday | 4 |
| Thursday | 5 |
| Friday | 10 |

The mean distance Jo walked last week was 6 km.

How far did Jo walk on Tuesday? **(3 marks)**

**B6.** Mr Patel asked every child in his class how many pens they have in their pencil case.

The bar chart shows some of the results.

Everyone owns at least one pen, and no-one owns more than five pens.

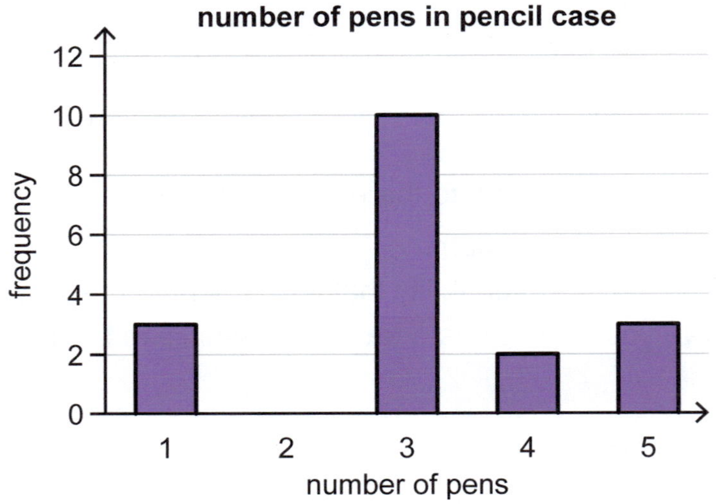


Five children own two pens.

**a)** Use this information to copy and complete the bar chart. **(1 mark)**

**b)** How many children are there altogether in Mr Patel's class? **(2 marks)**

**c)** How many pens in total do all the children in Mr Patel's class have? **(2 marks)**

A child is chosen at random.

**d)** Work out the probability the child has more than two pens. **(2 marks)**

**B7.** Max works in a school shop.

Max recorded the number of pieces of fruit sold each day last week.

The bar chart shows this information.

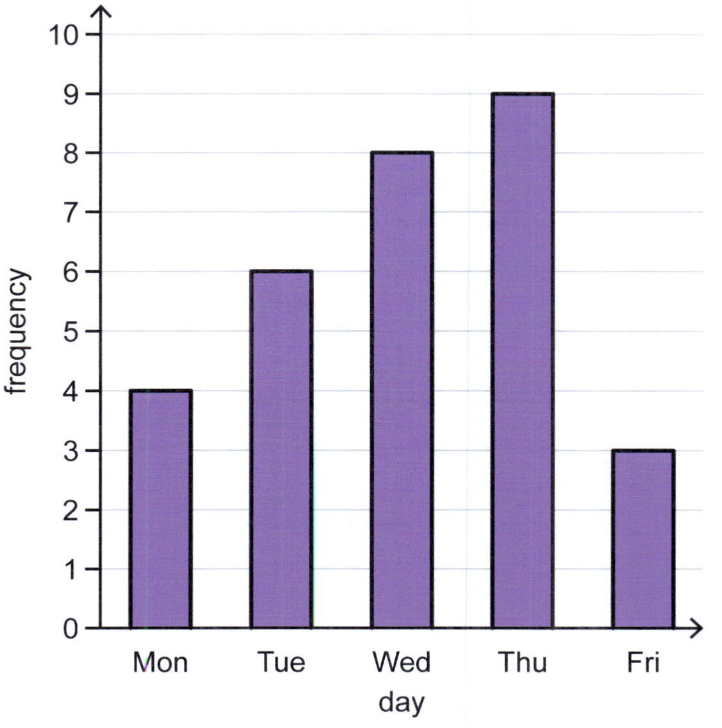


The total number of pieces of fruit sold last week is twice the total number of pieces of fruit sold on two of the days.

Which two days was this? **(3 marks)**

**B8.** The pictogram shows the number of boxes of chocolates sold each day last week in a shop.

The information for Sunday is missing.

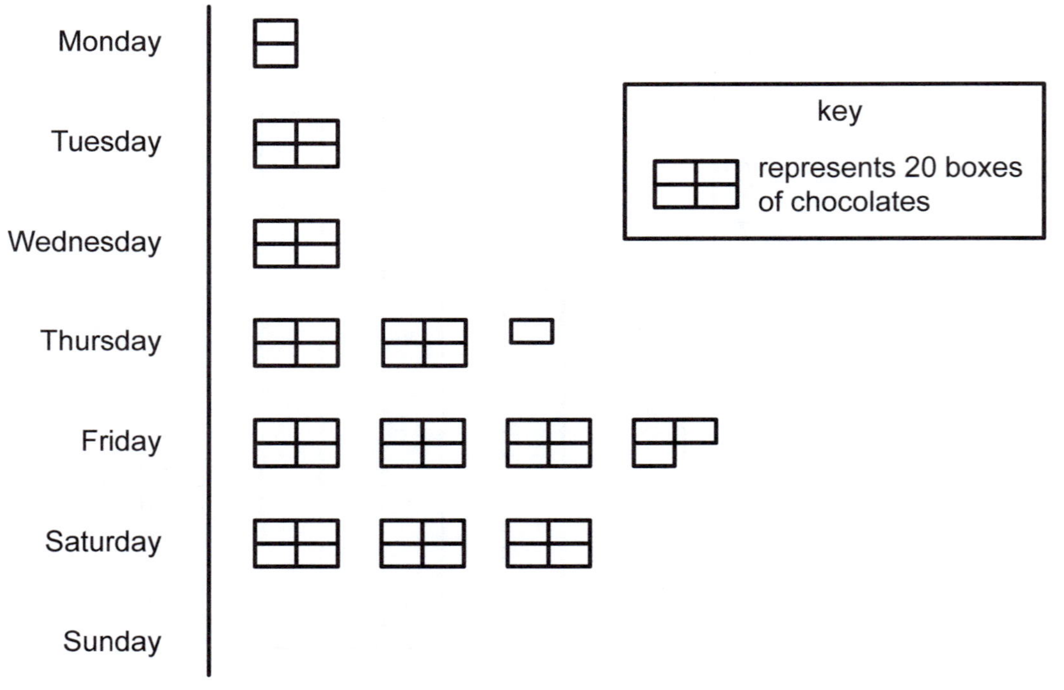


The mean number of boxes of chocolates sold last week is 40.

**a)** How many boxes of chocolates were sold on Sunday? **(2 marks)**

**b)** Draw the pictogram for Sunday. **(1 mark)**

**B9.** A holiday company asks 90 of its customers about which month they are more likely to travel during the summer.

The bar chart shows the results.

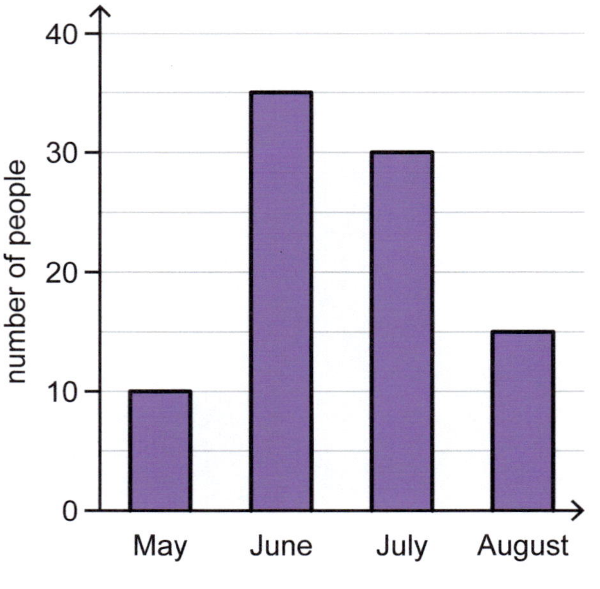

The company wants to draw a pie chart to represent the data.
Complete the table. **(3 marks)**

| Month | Number of customers | Angle in the pie chart |
|---|---|---|
| May | | |
| June | | |
| July | | |
| August | | |
| Total | 90 customers | 360° |

**B10.** The pie chart shows the results of 144 games played by a rugby team.
They lost a quarter of the games and drew and won an equal number of games.
Use these results to work out an estimate for the probability of the team winning a game.
Give your answer as a fraction in simplified form. **(5 marks)**

First, calculate the number of games they won.

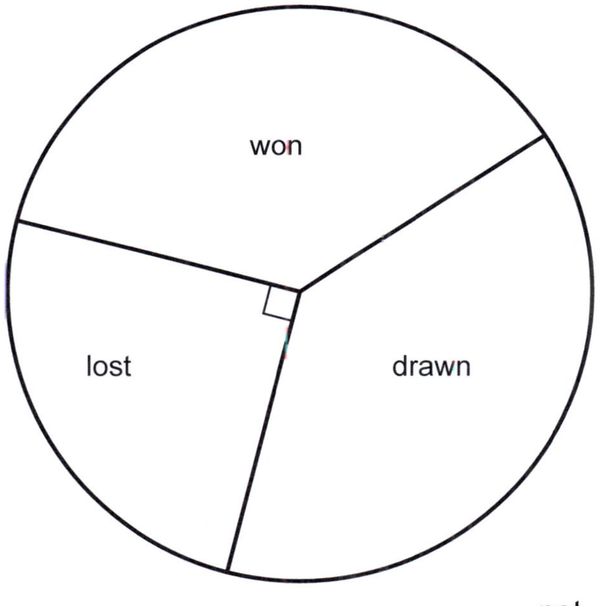


not drawn accurately

## Data Set C

**C1.** There are 13 children in a summer music club.
Four children play guitar and piano.
One child does not play guitar or piano.
Seven children play guitar.
How many children play piano? **(3 marks)**

Draw a Venn diagram.

**C2.** There are 19 runners in a long-distance race.
15 wear watches.
Six wear a hat.
One does not wear a watch or a hat.
A runner is chosen at random.
Work out the probability they wear a hat only. **(4 marks)**

Draw a Venn diagram.

**C3.** The pie chart shows information about the number of year 7 students in four local schools in a city.

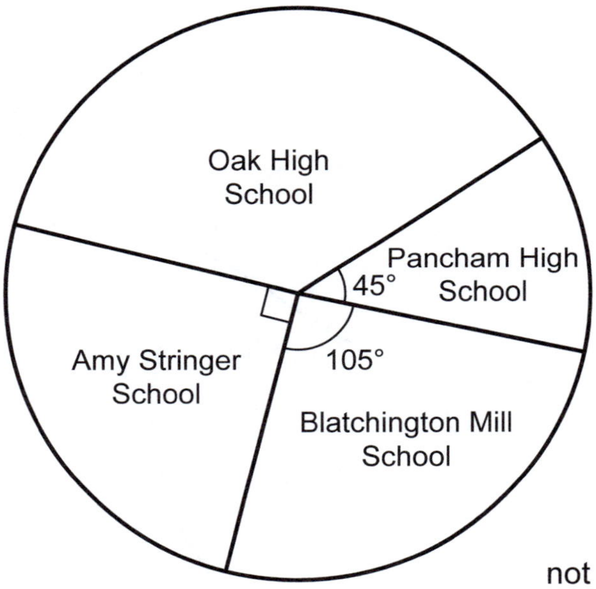


not drawn accurately

**a)** What fraction of the students went to Pancham High School? **(2 marks)**

60 children went to Pancham School.

**b)** How many students went to all four of the schools? **(2 marks)**

A student is chosen at random.

**c)** Work out the probability they did **not** go to Pancham High School. **(2 marks)**

Can you use the answer from part **a)**?

**C4.** The pie chart shows the activities that children did in a summer camp. Each child did one activity.

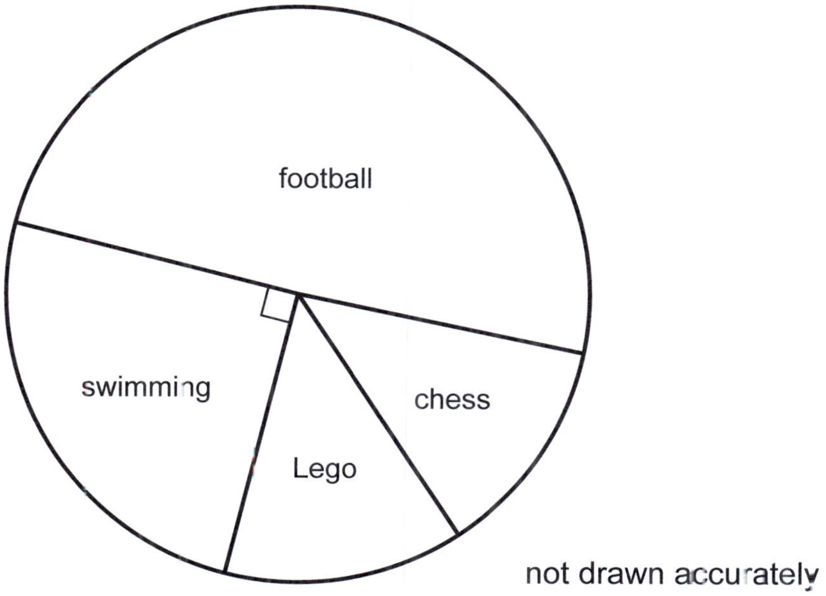


15 children went swimming.

How many children were there altogether in the summer camp? **(2 marks)**

**C5.** A group of children were asked what their favourite fruit was.

The pie chart shows the results.

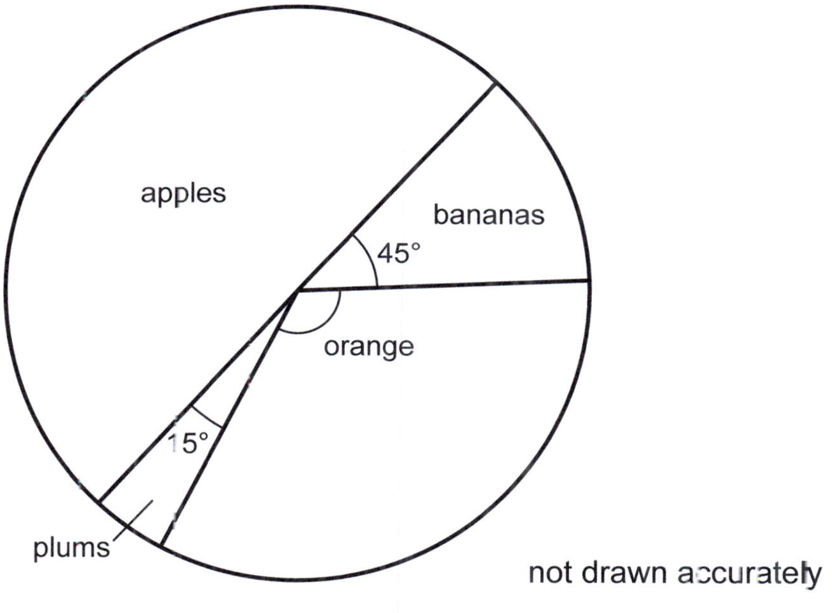


Half of the children said their favourite fruit were apples.

72 children said their favourite fruit was bananas.

**a)** Find the number of children whose favourite fruit was:

**i)** plums **(2 marks)**

**ii)** apples. **(2 marks)**

A child is chosen at random.

**b)** Work out the probability their favourite fruit is oranges. **(3 marks)**

**C6.** Kate asked some people to tell her their favourite colour.
Here is a pie chart showing the results.

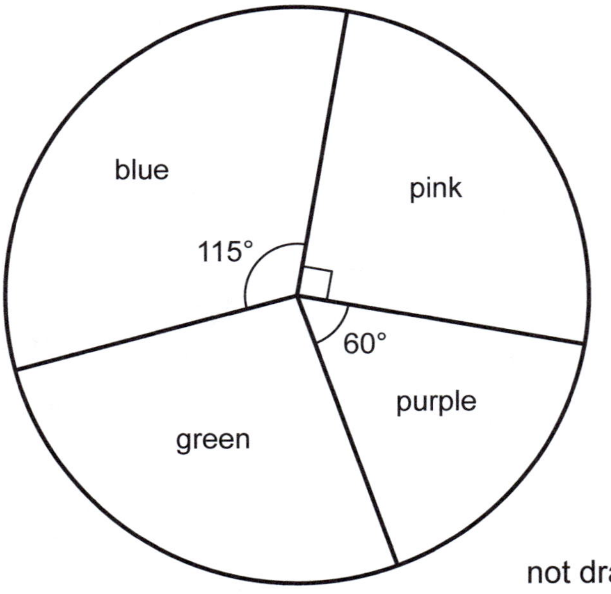


not drawn accurately

**a)** What percentage of the people like pink best? **(1 mark)**

**b)** What is the probability that a person likes purple best? **(2 marks)**

230 people like blue best.

**c)** How many people did Kate ask? **(2 marks)**

What fraction of the people like purple best?

**C7.** The pie chart shows information about how the students in Year 9 travel to school.

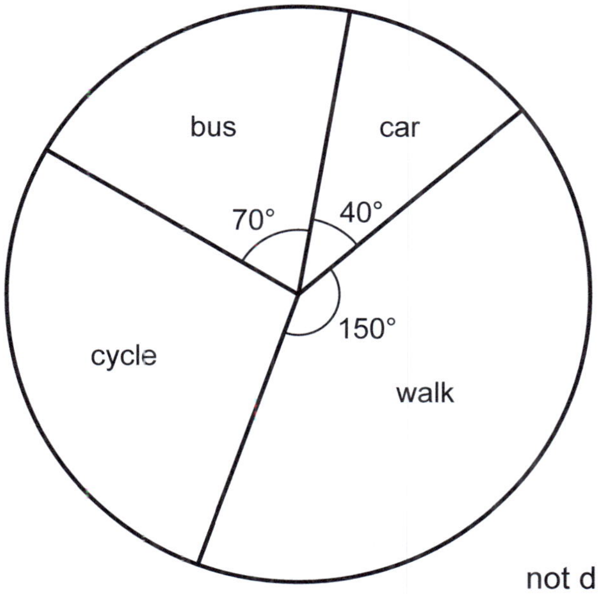


not drawn accurately

30 students walk to school.

**a)** How many students are there in Year 9? **(2 marks)**

A student is chosen at random.

**b)** Work out the probability they use the bus. **(2 marks)**

**C8.** There are only white counters, green counters, red counters and yellow counters in a bag.
The table shows each of the probabilities.

| **Colour** | white | green | red | yellow |
|---|---|---|---|---|
| **Probability** | 0.4 | 0.2 | | 0.25 |

One counter is picked up at random.

**a)** Work out the probability that it is a red counter. **(1 mark)**

There are 80 counters in the bag.

**b)** Work out the number of red counters in the bag. **(2 marks)**

**C9.** The school team is playing football on Monday.
The probability of rain on Monday is 0.4
The probability of winning at a football match if it rains is 0.3
The probability of winning at a football match if it does not rain is 0.65

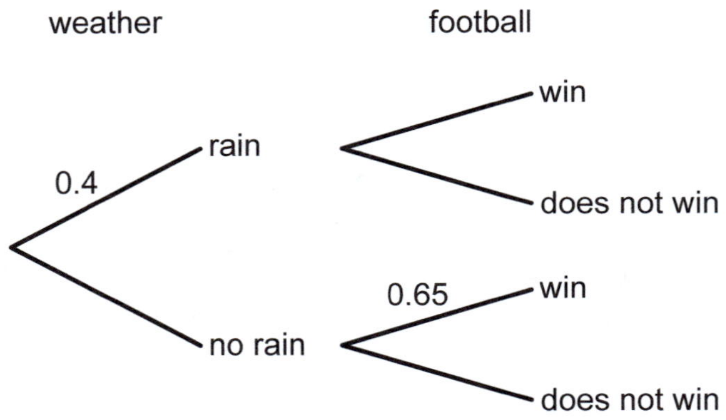


**a)** Copy and complete the diagram by writing the missing probabilities on each branch. **(2 marks)**

**b)** Work out the probability of the team winning the football match on Monday. **(2 marks)**

> Work out the probability of winning if it is raining.
> Work out the probability of winning if it is not raining.
> Add the probabilities together.

**C10.** There are a total of 90 students in Years 10 and 11.
42 of these students are in Year 10.
Eight of the Year 10 students cycle to school.
33 of the students cycle to school.

**a)** Use this information to complete the frequency tree. **(4 marks)**

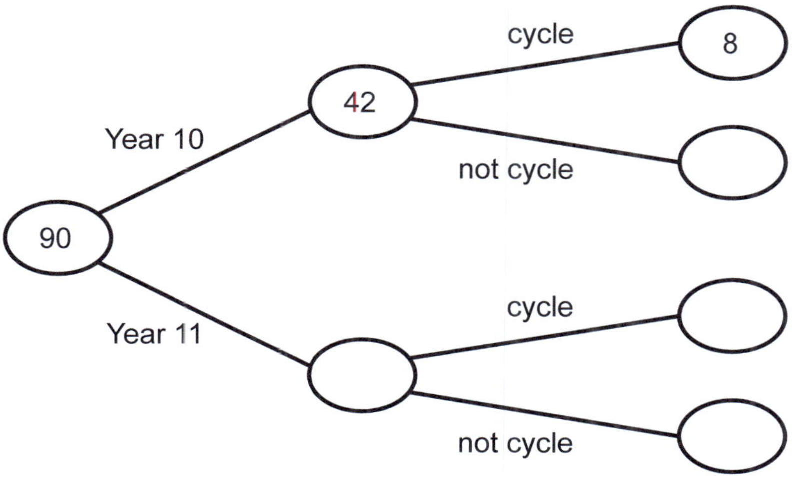


One of the Year 11 students is chosen at random.

**b)** Work out the probability that this student did **not** cycle. **(1 mark)**

## Data Set D

**D1.** Jake asks 37 people whether they own a cat or a dog.
21 people own a cat.
20 people own dog.
Five people do not own a cat or a dog.
How many people own either a cat or a dog, but not both? **(3 marks)**

Draw a Venn diagram.

**D2.** Some students go on a school trip to Europe.
Six students speak both French and German.
15 students speak French.
Eight students speak German only.
Three students do not speak German or French.

**a)** How many students go on the school trip? **(3 marks)**

A student is chosen at random.

**b)** Write down the probability that they speak German. **(1 mark)**

Draw a Venn diagram.

**D3** Miles has a 4-sided spinner.
The sides of the spinner are numbered 1, 2, 3 and 4.
The spinner is biased.
The table shows the probability of the spinner landing on each number.
The probability that the spinner will land on 3 is $x$.

| **Number** | 1 | 2 | 3 | 4 |
|---|---|---|---|---|
| **Probability** | 0.2 | $2x$ | $x$ | 0.35 |

**a)** Work out the probability that the spinner will land on 3. **(3 marks)**

Miles spins the spinner 80 times.

**b)** Work out an estimate for the number of times the spinner lands on 2. **(3 marks)**

**D4.** The table shows the number of goals that a school football team scored in each match last term.

| Number of goals | Number of matches |
|---|---|
| 0 | 3 |
| 1 | 4 |
| 2 | 5 |
| 3 | 4 |
| 4 | 2 |
| 5 | 1 |
| 6 | 1 |

**a)** How many matches did the team play in total? **(2 marks)**

**b)** How many goals did the team score in total? **(2 marks)**

**c)** Find the mean number of goals per match last term. **(1 mark)**

**D5.** Jasmine records the length of her three favourite songs.

| Song | Length |
|---|---|
| Song 1 | 3 minutes 45 seconds |
| Song 2 | 2 minutes 40 seconds |
| Song 3 | 3 minutes 5 seconds |

What is the mean (average) length of the songs?
Give your answer in minutes and seconds. **(3 marks)**

**D6.** There are twelve students from Year 10 and ten students from Year 11 in the swimming club.

The mean height of the Year 10 students is 158 cm.

The mean height of all the students is 160 cm.

What is the mean height of the Year 11 students? **(3 marks)**

**D7.** This frequency table records the length of time the school bus was late in the morning last month.

| **Length of time (minutes)** | 0 | 1 | 2 | 3 | 4 | 5 | 6 |
|---|---|---|---|---|---|---|---|
| **Frequency** | 13 | 5 | 4 | 1 | 2 | 3 | 2 |

**a)** How many days was the bus more than 2 minutes late? **(1 mark)**

**b)** What is the mean (average) number of minutes the bus was late last month? **(3 marks)**

**c)** What is the median length of time? **(1 mark)**

**d)** What is the range of the length of time? **(1 mark)**

**e)** What is the modal length of time? **(1 mark)**

**D8.** The table shows the number of computers sold in a shop on each of five days.

| **Day** | Mon | Tue | Wed | Thu | Fri |
|---|---|---|---|---|---|
| **Number of computers sold** | 5 | 12 | 11 | 5 | 8 |

Marion uses this information to draw this bar chart.

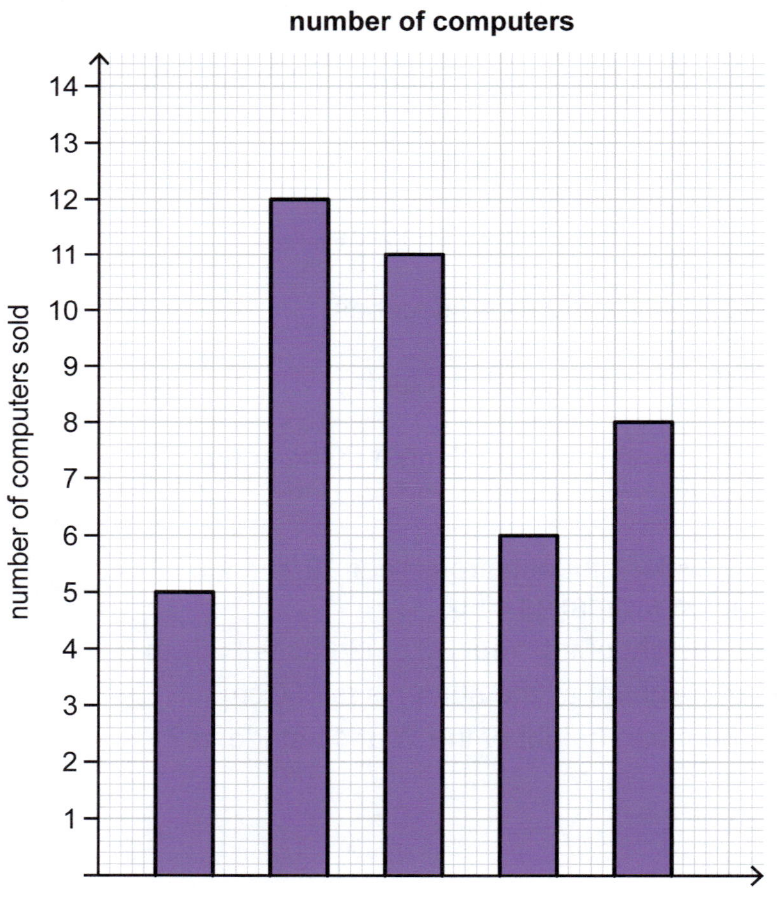


State **three** things that are incorrect about this bar chart, and describe what should be done to fix each error. **(3 marks)**

**D9.** Alison draws a scatter diagram to show the heights and masses of ten chimpanzees.

Alison plots the points accurately, and then draws a line of best fit.

State **three** things that are incorrect about this diagram, and describe what should be done to fix each error. **(3 marks)**

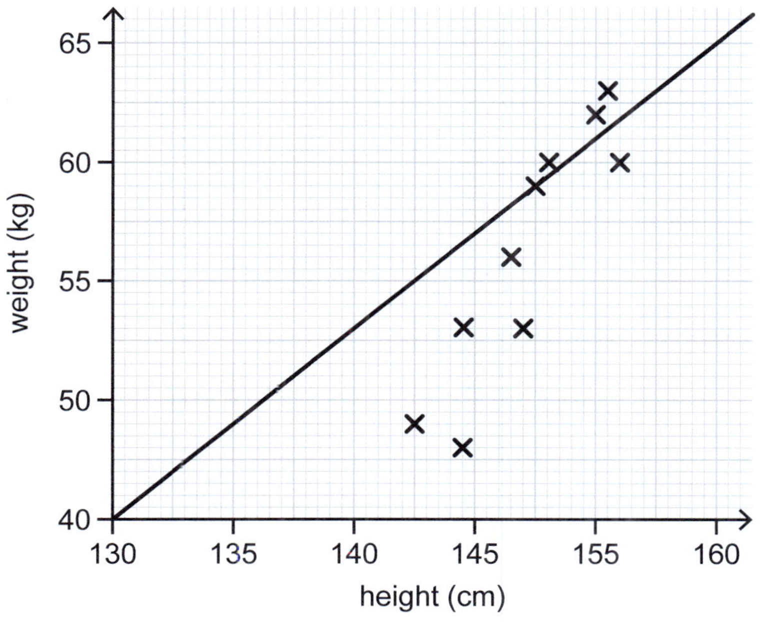


**D10.** The table shows some information about the masses of some cucumbers.

Amy drew the frequency polygon below to show the information in the table.

State **three** things that are incorrect about this diagram, and describe what should be done to fix each error. **(3 marks)**

| Mass, $w$ (g) | Frequency |
|---|---|
| $15 < w \leqslant 20$ | 8 |
| $20 < w \leqslant 30$ | 21 |
| $30 < w \leqslant 40$ | 13 |
| $40 < w \leqslant 50$ | 7 |
| $50 < w \leqslant 60$ | 3 |

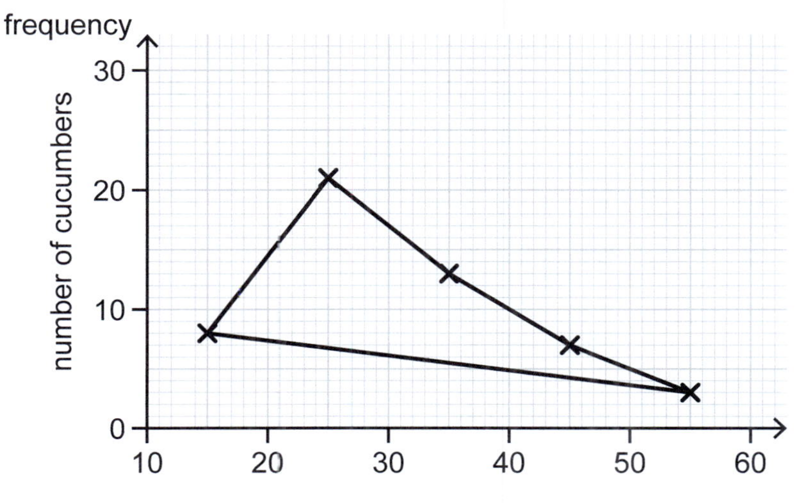

## Data Set E

**E1.** Beth has three cards.
Each card has a number on it.
The numbers are hidden.

The mode of the three numbers is 7.
The mean of the three numbers is 6.
Work out the range of the numbers on the cards. **(4 marks)**

**E2.** Here is a probability tree diagram.

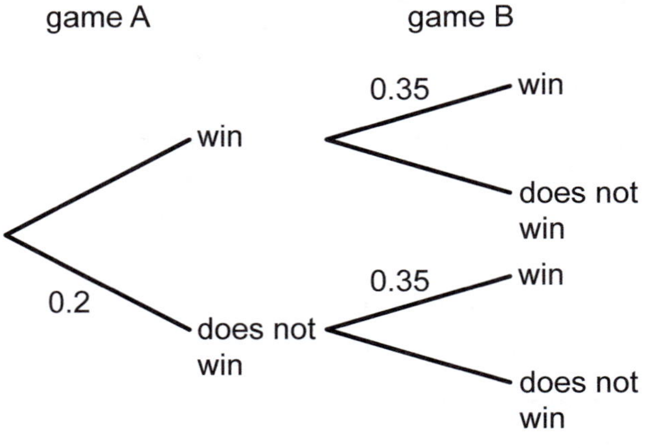


**a)** Copy and complete the diagram by writing the missing probabilities on each branch. **(3 marks)**

**b)** Work out the probability of winning both games. **(2 marks)**

**E3.** Here are the ages, in years, of 20 people living in Barnfield Road.

| | | | | | | | | | |
|---|---|---|---|---|---|---|---|---|---|
| 13 | 32 | 25 | 41 | 23 | 26 | 28 | 29 | 32 | 30 |
| 21 | 13 | 40 | 35 | 34 | 28 | 32 | 19 | 27 | 31 |

Amber drew this stem and leaf diagram to show this information.

| | | | | | | | |
|---|---|---|---|---|---|---|---|
| 1 | 3 | 3 | 9 | | | | |
| 2 | 1 | 3 | 5 | 6 | 7 | 8 | 9 |
| 3 | 0 | 1 | 2 | 2 | 2 | 5 | 4 |
| 4 | 0 | 1 | | | | | |

Key: 1|3 represents 13 people

State **three** things that are incorrect about this diagram, and describe what should be done to fix each error. **(3 marks)**

**E4.** The stem and leaf diagram gives information about the heights of 25 players in the football team.

| | | | | | | | | |
|---|---|---|---|---|---|---|---|---|
| 14 | 5 | 7 | 7 | 9 | | | | |
| 15 | 2 | 2 | 3 | 5 | 6 | 8 | | |
| 16 | 0 | 1 | 4 | 6 | 7 | 8 | 9 | 0 |
| 17 | 1 | 2 | 2 | 6 | 7 | | | |
| 18 | 0 | 3 | | | | | | |

Key:
14|5 represents 145 cm

**a)** Find the median height. **(1 mark)**

Archie says that more than 20% of the 25 players have a height greater than 172 cm.

**b)** Is Archie correct? You must show how you get your answer **(2 marks)**

What is 20% of 25?
How many players are **taller than** 172 cm?

**E5.** The table gives information about the number of minutes Aran went cycling each day in April.

| Number of minutes, $M$ | Frequency |
|---|---|
| $0 \leqslant M < 30$ | 5 |
| $30 \leqslant M < 60$ | 6 |
| $60 \leqslant M < 90$ | |
| $90 \leqslant M < 120$ | 9 |
| $120 \leqslant M < 150$ | |

The ratio of
(Frequency for $60 \leqslant M < 90$) : (Frequency for $120 \leqslant M < 150$)
is 4 : 1

**a)** Complete the frequency table. **(2 marks)**

**b)** Work out an estimate for the mean number of hours Aran went cycling in April. **(4 marks)**

Find the midpoint for each interval.

Alan's coach chose one day in April at random in order to study Alan's training.

**c)** Find the probability that Alan cycled for less than 60 minutes on the day his coach chose. Give your answer as a fraction. **(2 marks)**

**E6.** Hannah asks a group of 21 students whether they study Physics or Chemistry.

Five students study Chemistry.

15 students study Physics.

One student studies both Chemistry and Physics.

Work out the probability that a student chosen at random does not study Chemistry or Physics. **(4 marks)**

**E7.** 200 passengers travel from City Airport to Rome or Milan in either economy or business class on Monday morning.

Of these 200 passengers

- 41 travel business class to Rome
- 89 travel economy class to Milan
- 130 travel economy class.

**a)** Copy the two-way table and use the information to complete it. **(4 marks)**

| | Rome | Milan | Total |
|---|---|---|---|
| **Business class** | | | |
| **Economy class** | | | |
| **Total** | | | |

A person is chosen at random.

**b)** Work out the probability that they travel economy class to Rome. **(1 mark)**

**E8.** These are the number of goals a football team scored in the last 9 games.

1, 0, 2, 3, $x$, $x$ , 5, 2, 2

The mean number of goals is 3.

Work out the median number of goals. **(3 marks)**

**E9.** Charlotte works as a taxi driver.

From Monday to Friday the mean distance she drove was 102 km per day.

For the 7 days from Monday to Sunday the mean distance she drove was 128 km per day.

Charlotte drove 135 km on Saturday

How far did she drive on Sunday? **(4 marks)**

What is the formula to work out the mean?

**E10.** There are 80 people in the school canteen.

18 of these people are teachers.

The rest are students.

37 of the 80 people are vegetarian.

Four of the teachers are vegetarian.

**a)** Use this information to copy and complete the frequency tree. **(4 marks)**

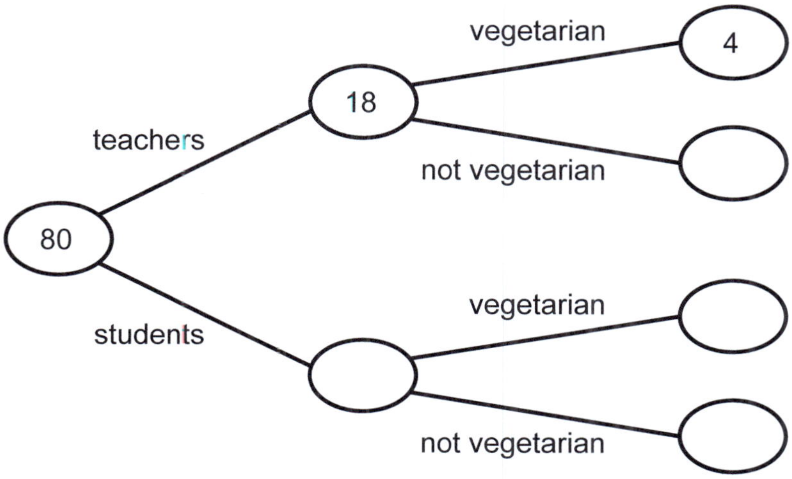


One of the students is chosen at random.

**b)** Find the probability that they are not vegetarian. **(1 mark)**

# End of Chapter Notes

You could try and complete the 10 questions in each set, in a single study session. This may help with exam practice and keeping the focus going even when the questions are challenging.

| |
|---|
| 1. |
| 2. |
| 3. |

Write 3 things you feel you need to keep an eye on.

| |
|---|
| 1. |
| 2. |
| 3. |

Write 3 common mistakes that either you or your friends may make.

You could write specific mistakes or whole questions that you feel are easy to make a mistake on.

| |
|---|
| 1. |
| 2. |
| 3. |

## Well done for completing this chapter!

# Chapter 5
# Mixed Questions

*"Courage doesn't always roar. Sometimes courage is the quiet voice at the end of the day saying, 'I will try again tomorrow." – Mary Anne Radmacher*

**Worked Solutions**

**The diagrams in all the questions are not drawn accurately. This means you need to work out the answers by calculating, not measuring.**

## Mixed questions Set A

**A1.** Jamal wraps some parcels.

He wraps 2 large parcels and 3 small parcels.

For each large parcel he uses $x$ centimetres of wrapping paper.

For each small parcel he uses $p$ centimetres of wrapping paper.

**a)** Write an expression for the total, $T$ in centimetres, of the wrapping paper that Jamal uses. **(2 marks)**

In total Jamal uses 7 metres of wrapping paper.

He uses 112 cm of wrapping paper for each small parcel.

**b)** Work out the amount of wrapping paper Jamal uses for each large parcel. **(3 marks)**

**A2.** The bar chart shows information about the number of jars of jam sold at a market.

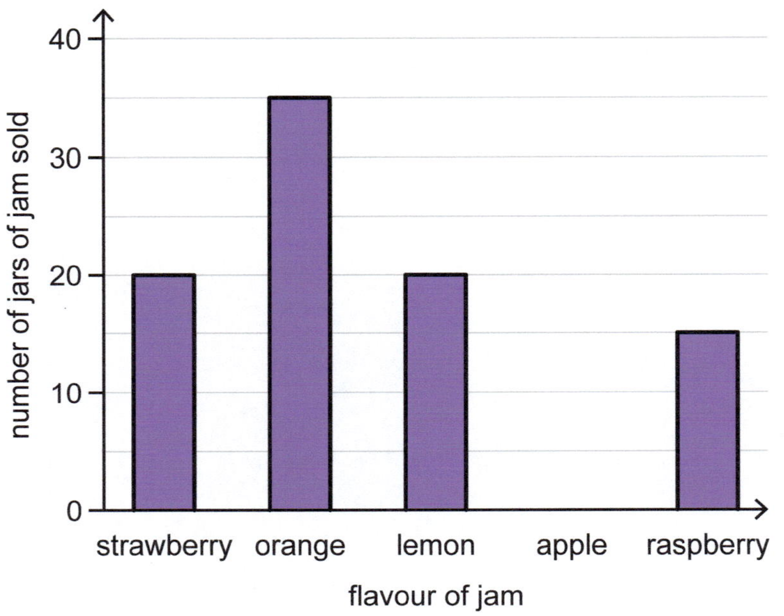


The ratio of the number of jars of strawberry : apple is 4 : 5.

**a)** Draw a bar for 'Apple' on the bar chart. **(3 marks)**

**b)** Find the ratio of the number of jars of orange : raspberry. **(2 marks)**

Xavi says, 'There are 5 different jams sold in the market today.

The probability of selling strawberry jam is $\frac{1}{5}$.'

**c)** Use the bar chart to state whether or not Xavi is correct. Give reasons for your answer. **(2 marks)**

**A3.** Tom's teacher gives him a number $x$.

She tells him that 5% of $x$ is 20.

Tom thinks that $\frac{1}{5}$ of $x$ is $20 \div 5 = 4$.

Tom is incorrect.

Find the correct value for $\frac{1}{5}$ of $x$. **(2 marks)**

**A4.** Here is the price list for a school stationery shop.

| | |
|---|---|
| pens: | £1.20 for a pack of 6 |
| pencils: | 85p for a pack of 15 |
| rulers: | 90p for a pack of 3 |
| pencil cases: | 65p each |

Alba buys 30 pens, 30 pencils, 30 rulers and 30 pencil cases.

Find the total amount of money Alba spends. **(3 marks)**

**A5.** It takes 30 minutes to fill a swimming pool with water using 4 taps.

**a)** How long would it take if 5 taps were used? **(2 marks)**

**b)** State the assumption you made in part **a**. **(1 mark)**

**A6.** Ava has to paint some cylindrical tins.

She paints all the surfaces.

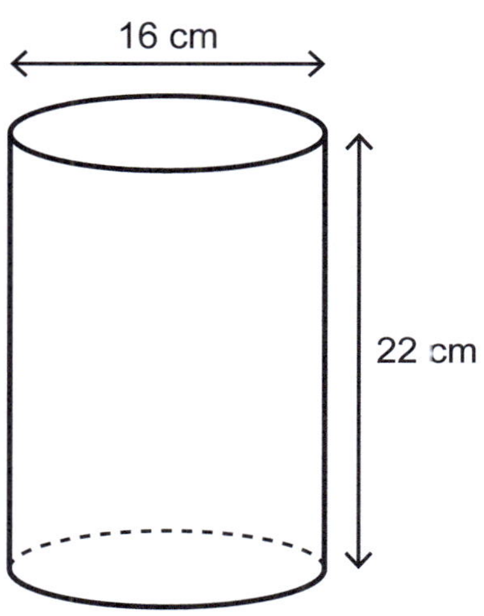


area of circle = $\pi r^2$
curved surface area of cylinder = $2\pi rh$

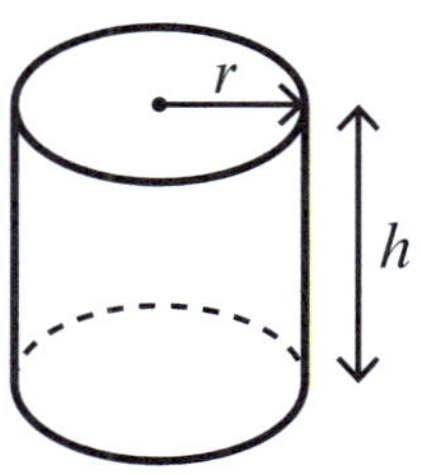


Each tin has a diameter of 16 cm and a height of 22 cm.

Ava has 10 tubes of paint.

Each tube covers 350 cm$^2$.

How many complete tins can Ava paint? **(5 marks)**

**A7.** There are 28 students in class 11C.

20 of the students play football.

17 of the students play tennis.

One student does not play either sport.

**a)** How many students play tennis only? **(3 marks)**

Draw a Venn diagram.

**b)** A student is chosen at random from class 11C.

Work out the probability that this student plays both tennis and football. **(1 mark)**

**A8.** Harry invests £300 for 3 years.

He gets simple interest of 4% per year.

Work out the total interest Harry gets at the end of the three years. **(3 marks)**

**A9.** Here is the list of ingredients for making a tray of 30 biscuits.

| **Ingredients for 30 biscuits** |
|---|
| 225 g butter |
| 150 g sugar |
| 275 g flour |
| 125 g chocolate chips |

Lucas has 900 g of butter, 500 g of caster sugar, 1 kg of plain flour and 250 g of chocolate chips.

What is the maximum number of biscuits he can make? **(3 marks)**

**A10.** The diagram shows a table mat in the shape of a rectangle.
All measurements are in centimetres.

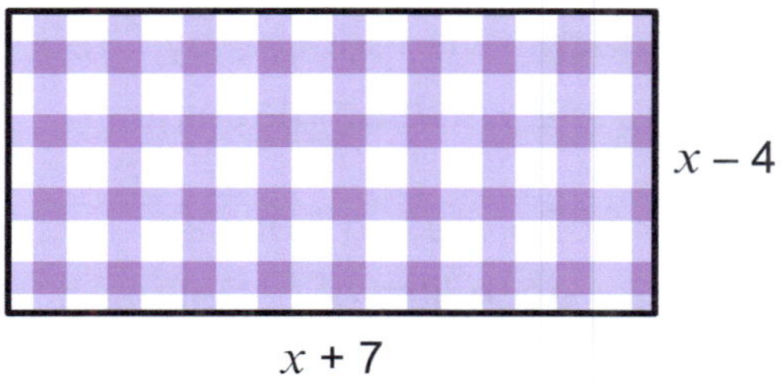


The perimeter of the table mat is 126 cm.

**a)** Show that $2x + 3 = 63$ **(3 marks)**

**b)** Hence find the area of the table mat. **(4 marks)**

## Mixed questions Set B

**B1.** In a sale, prices are reduced by 20%.
The price of a washing machine is reduced by £136.
Work out the sale price of the washing machine. **(3 marks)**

**B2.** In October Maria drove 660 miles in her car.
The car travelled 12 km for each litre of petrol used.
Petrol costs £1.30 per litre.
Work out the cost of the petrol Maria used in October.
Use the approximate conversion 5 miles = 8 km. **(4 marks)**

**B3.** The table shows the number of penalties each footballer in the school squad has scored.

| Number of penalties | Frequency |
|---|---|
| 0 | 2 |
| 1 | 7 |
| 2 | 6 |
| 3 | 11 |
| 4 | 1 |
| 5 | 2 |

**a)** Work out the range of the number of penalties. **(1 mark)**

**b)** Write down the mode of the penalties scored. **(1 mark)**

**c)** Work out the mean of the number of penalties scored.
Give your answer to the nearest whole number. **(3 marks)**

**B4.** A shop sells boxes of teas.
Each box of tea costs £4.
Matilda has £27.

**a)** Work out the number of boxes of tea Matilda can buy. **(2 marks)**

In a sale, boxes of teas are sold at half price. Matilda thinks she can now buy exactly twice the number of tea boxes for £27.

**b)** Is Matilda correct? You must give a reason for your answer. **(1 mark)**

**B5.** Here is a number machine.

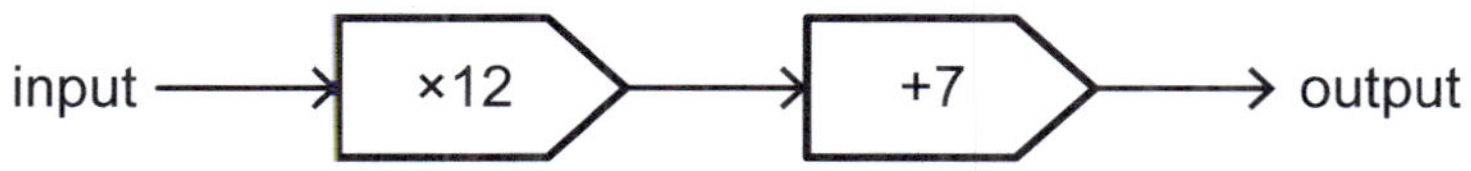


**a)** Work out the output when the input is 9.

Here is a different number machine.

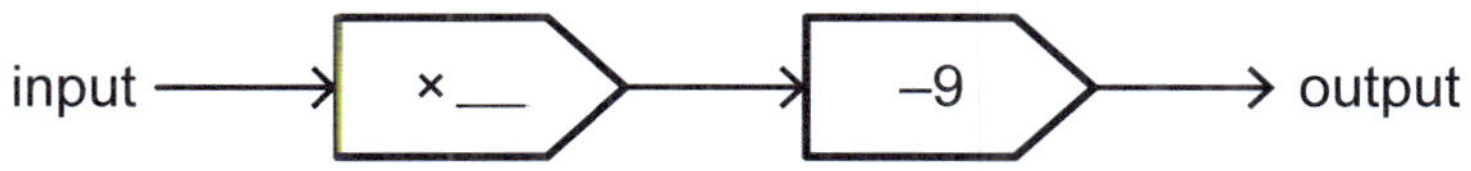


When the input is 6, the output is 87.

**b)** What number is missing from the number machine? **(2 marks)**

**B6.** The stem and leaf diagram shows the height of 21 trees in Verulanium Park.
The heights have been measured to the nearest 10 cm.

| | | | | | | |
|---|---|---|---|---|---|---|
| 10 | 0 | 2 | 9 | | | |
| 11 | 1 | 1 | 3 | 5 | 7 | |
| 12 | 2 | 4 | 5 | 7 | 8 | 9 |
| 13 | 6 | 6 | 7 | 9 | | |
| 14 | 0 | 0 | 1 | | | |

Key: 10|2 represents 10.2 m

**a)** Find the median height. **(1 mark)**

The trees in Abbotts Hill Park have a median height of 10.1 m.

Their heights have a range of 5.9 m.

**b)** Compare the distribution of the heights of the trees in Verulanium Park with the distribution of the heights of the trees in Abbotts Hill Park. **(4 marks)**

**B7.** Finn invests £4500 in a savings account for 3 years.
The account pays simple interest at a rate of 1.2% per year.
Work out the total amount of interest Finn gets by the end of the 3 years. **(2 marks)**

**B8.** The diagram shows a scale drawing of the tennis court in the local gym.

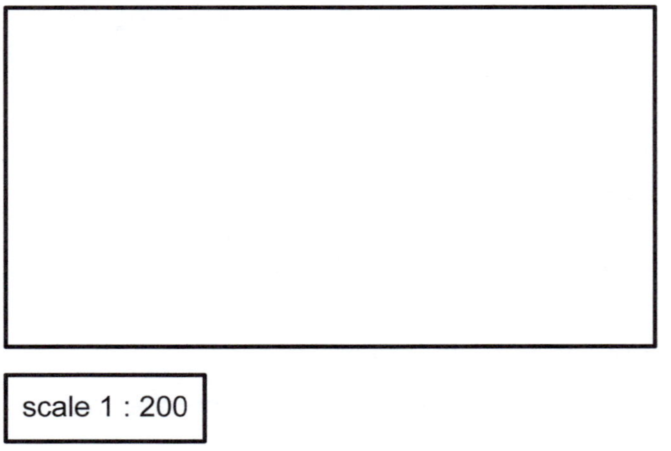


The ratio of length : width is 2 : 1.

The perimeter of the drawing of the tennis court is 36 cm.

The scale of the drawing is 1 : 200.

Work out the length of the real tennis court.

Give your answer in metres. **(5 marks)**

**B9** Here is some information about the sports played by members of a sports club.

92 people are members of the club.

45 members play cricket.

32 members play badminton.

14 members play cricket and badminton.

**a)** Complete the Venn diagram to show this information. **(3 marks)**

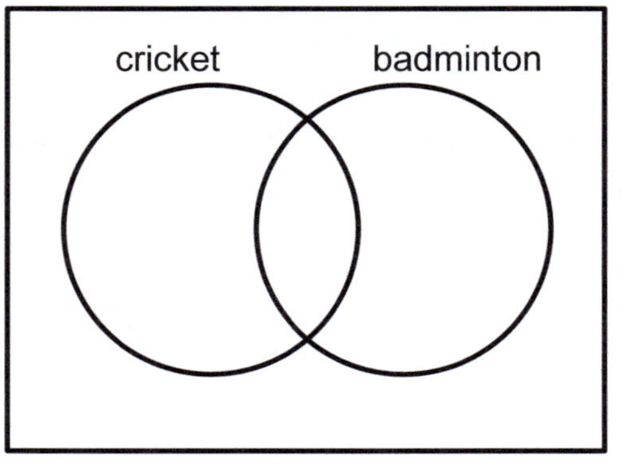


A member is chosen at random.

**b)** Work out probability that they do not play badminton and they do not play cricket. **(1 mark)**

**B10.** Kirsty is planning a trip to a theme park for one adult and two children.
These are the costs for the trip.

| | |
|---|---|
| Train tickets | £28 for each adult<br>£4.50 for each child |
| Tickets to theme park | £32 for each adult<br>£22.50 for each child |
| Meals | £16 for each adult<br>£10 for each child |

Kirsty has £85 to spend.
How much more money does she need to pay for the trip? **(5 marks)**

## Mixed questions Set C

**C1.** Melissa wants to increase 200 by 4%.

She writes down:

200 × 1.4 = 280

**a)** Melissa's method is wrong. Explain why. **(1 mark)**

Jake wants to decrease 150 by 3%. He writes down

1 – 0.3 = 0.7

150 × 0.7 = 105

**b)** Jake's method is wrong. Explain why. **(1 mark)**

**C2.** Tyrol bakes and sells cakes.

The pictogram shows information about the number of cakes that he baked from Monday to Thursday last week.

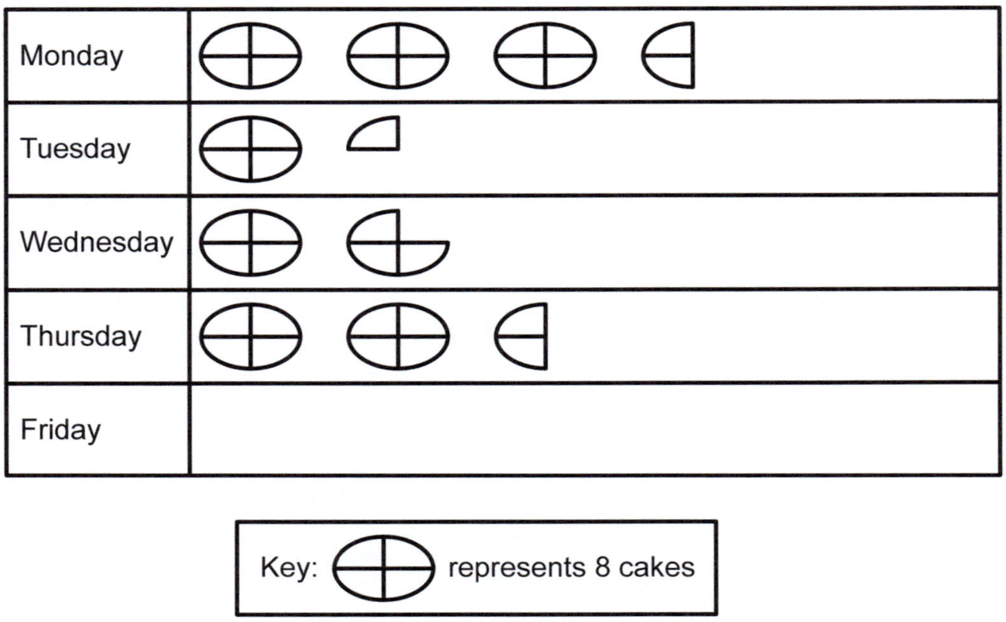


**a)** How many cakes did he bake on Tuesday? **(1 mark)**

Tyrol baked 20 cakes on Friday.

**b)** Show this information on the pictogram. **(2 marks)**

Tyrol sells the cakes for £18 each. It costs him £4.50 to make a cake.

**c)** Work out the amount of profit that Tyrol made from Monday to Friday last week. **(5 marks)**

**C3.** Three positive whole numbers have a median of 7, a mode of 7 and a mean of 5.

Find the range of these numbers. **(3 marks)**

**C4.** Find the smallest angle in this triangle.

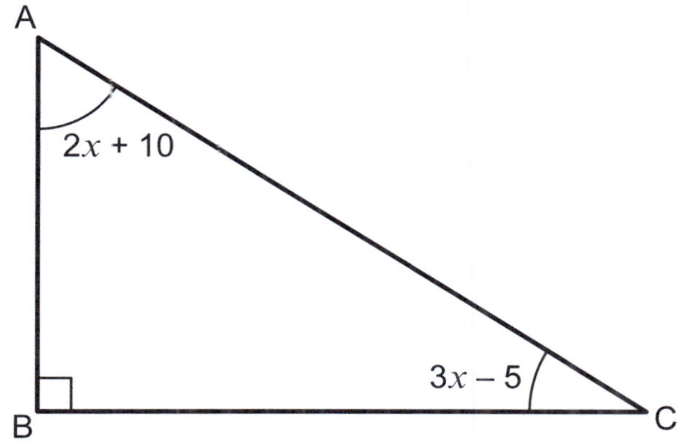


The angles in a triangle add up to 180°. Use this to form an equation in $x$, and solve it.

**C5.** Tom buys 60 calculators for £4.50 each.

He sells $\frac{3}{5}$ of the calculators for £7 each.

He sells the rest of the calculators for £5.

Work out Tom's profit. **(5 marks)**

**C6.** Ben wants to invest £25 000 for 3 years in a bank.

| **Personal Bank** | **Secure Bank** |
|---|---|
| Compound Interest | Compound Interest |
| 2% for each year | 3.5% for the first year with an additional 1% for each extra year |

Which bank will give Ben the most interest?
You must show all your working. **(6 marks)**

**C7.** Charlie runs every day.

Here are the distances, in miles, she ran in the last 7 days.

The distances are written in order of size.

2, 2, 5, 6, $x$, 11, 13

**a)** Find the range of the distances that Charlie ran. **(1 mark)**

**b)** Find the median distance that Charlie ran. **(1 mark)**

The mean daily distance that Charlie ran was 7 miles per day.

**c)** Work out the value of $x$. **(3 marks)**

**C8.** Alicia makes a scale model of an aeroplane.

She uses a scale of 1 : 75

The length of Alicia's model aeroplane is 66 cm.

Mazar makes a scale model of the same aeroplane.

He uses a scale of 1 : 50

Work out the length of Mazar's model aeroplane. **(3 marks)**

**C9.** There are 10 slices of pizza in each small pizza.

There are 12 slices of pizza in each large pizza.

George buys $s$ small pizzas and $l$ large pizzas.

He buys a total of $T$ slices of pizza.

Write a formula for $T$ in terms of $s$ and $l$. **(3 marks)**

**C10.** There are 32 biscuits in a jar.

$\frac{3}{8}$ of them are dark chocolate and the rest are milk chocolate.

Each biscuit is either in the shape of a star or a rectangle.

There are 8 biscuits that are dark chocolate and in the shape of a star.

The ratio **number of stars : number of rectangles** is 5 : 11

**a)** Copy and complete the table. **(5 marks)**

| | Milk chocolate | Dark chocolate | Total |
|---|---|---|---|
| **Star shape** | | | |
| **Rectangular shape** | | | |
| **Total** | | | |

**b)** Work out the ratio of rectangular milk chocolate biscuits to rectangular dark chocolate biscuits.

Give your answer as a ratio in its simplest form. **(1 mark)**

## Mixed questions Set D

**D1.** 2 kg of apples cost £3.50.

**a)** How much will 5 kg of apples cost? **(2 marks)**

The ratio of the price of 1 kg of apples : 1 kg of cherries is 1 : 2.

**b)** How much will 1.5 kg of cherries cost? **(2 marks)**

**D2.** Amy invests £2000 for 7 years at $x$% simple interest per year.
At the end of the 7 years, Amy receives a total of £350 in interest.
Work out the value of $x$. **(3 marks)**

**D3.** The table shows the number of cousins that 30 children have.

| Number of cousins | Frequency |
|---|---|
| 0 | 4 |
| 1 | 5 |
| 2 | 5 |
| 3 | 8 |
| 4 | $x$ |
| 5 | 3 |

**a)** Work out the number of children that had 4 cousins. **(1 mark)**

**b)** Work out the mean number of cousins per child. Give your answer to one decimal place. **(3 marks)**

**D4.** The diagram shows a right-angled triangle and a rectangle.

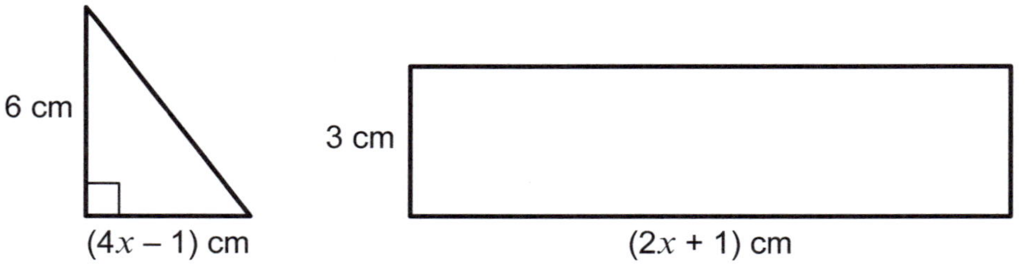


The area of the rectangle is twice the area of the triangle.

**a)** Work out the value of $x$. **(4 marks)**

**b)** Find the area of the rectangle. **(2 marks)**

**D5.** Kerim buys a car for £8000.

The value of the car depreciates by 12% each year.

Work out the value of the car at the end of 3 years. **(3 marks)**

What is the multiplier when the value of the car decreases by 12%?

**D6.** The table shows information about snowfall in the mountains in Italy in December one year.

| **Snowfall, $s$ (cm)** | **Frequency** |
|---|---|
| $0 \leqslant s < 2$ | 2 |
| $2 \leqslant s < 4$ | $x$ |
| $4 \leqslant s < 6$ | $y$ |
| $6 \leqslant s < 8$ | 6 |
| $8 \leqslant s < 10$ | 8 |
| $10 \leqslant s < 12$ | 1 |

The ratio of $x : y = 3 : 4$.

**a)** Find $x$ and $y$. **(4 marks)**

How many days are there in December?

**b)** Work out the mean snowfall in December.
Give your answer correct to one decimal place. **(4 marks)**

**D7.** Vinny invests £200 000 in a savings account for 4 years.

The account pays compound interest at a rate of 1.5 % per annum.

Calculate the total amount of interest Vinny will get at the end of 4 years. **(3 marks)**

**D8.** A box of chocolates contains 28 chocolates.
Each chocolate is either mint chocolate or dark chocolate.
All chocolates has either a nut centre or a toffee centre.
There are 6 mint chocolates with a nut centre.
There are 11 dark chocolates altogether.
There are 15 toffees altogether.

**a)** Copy and complete the frequency tree diagram. **(3 marks)**

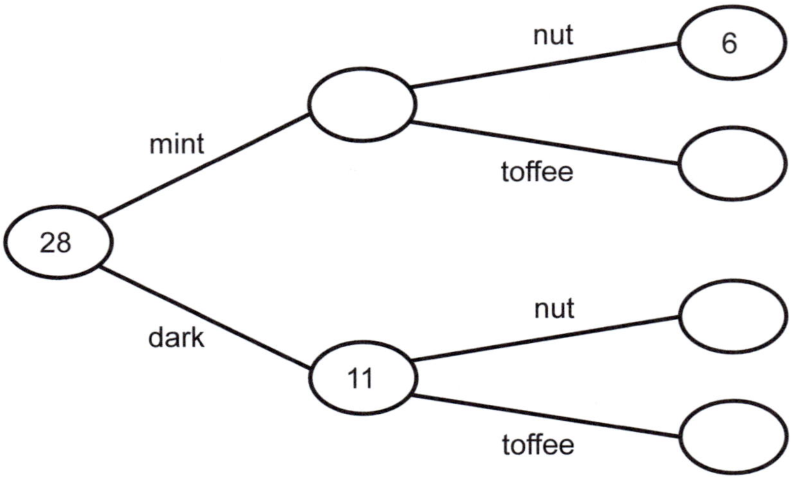


A chocolate is chosen at random.

**b)** Work out the probability of it being dark chocolate with a nut centre.
Give your answer as a fraction in simplified form. **(2 marks)**

**D9.** The side lengths of a right-angled triangle are given in the diagram.
The perimeter of the triangle is 24 cm.

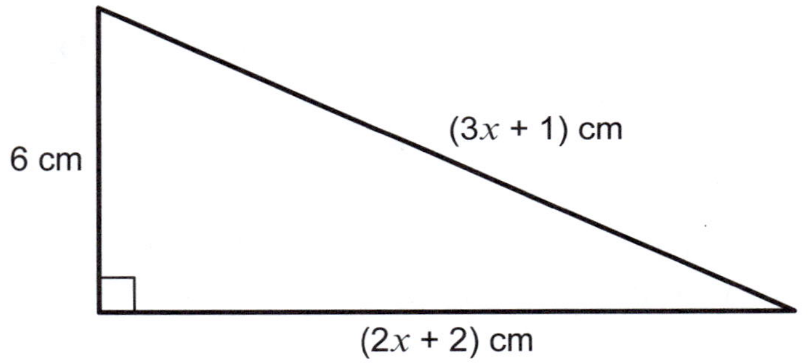


**a)** Find the value of $x$. **(3 marks)**

**b)** Find the area of the triangle. **(2 marks)**

**D10.** There are 10 counters in a bag. 3 counters are red and 7 are blue.

Lucas picks a counter at random. He writes down the colour and then replaces the counter in the bag.

He then picks a second counter and writes down its colour.

**a)** Copy and complete the tree diagram to show the probabilities of Lucas picking a particular colour of counter.
Give each probability as a fraction. **(2 marks)**

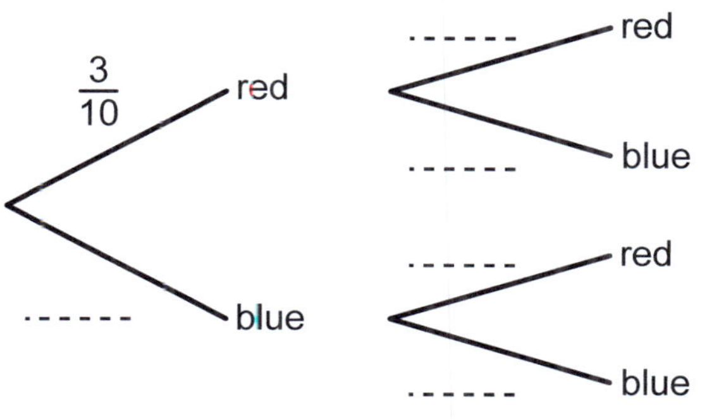


**b)** Work out the probability that Lucas picks two counters that are the same colour. Give your answers as a fraction in simplest form. **(4 marks)**

## Mixed questions Set E

**E1.** The price of a new calculator has increased by 24%.
The price of the calculator has increased by £3.60.
Work out the original price. **(3 marks)**

**E2.** Amir shares some money with his sister Gemini in the ratio 3 : 5.
Amir gets £4.50.
How much more money does Gemini receive than Amir? **(3 marks)**

**E3.** There are 14 dogs in a park.
Eight are golden retrievers.
The rest are labradors.
Six dogs are on a lead.
Three golden retrievers are not on a lead.
How many labradors are not on a lead? **(4 marks)**

Use the table to help you.

| | **Golden retriever** | **Labrador** | **Total** |
|---|---|---|---|
| **On a lead** | | | |
| **Not on a lead** | | | |
| **Total** | | | |

**E4.** The length of a rectangle is twice as long as its width.

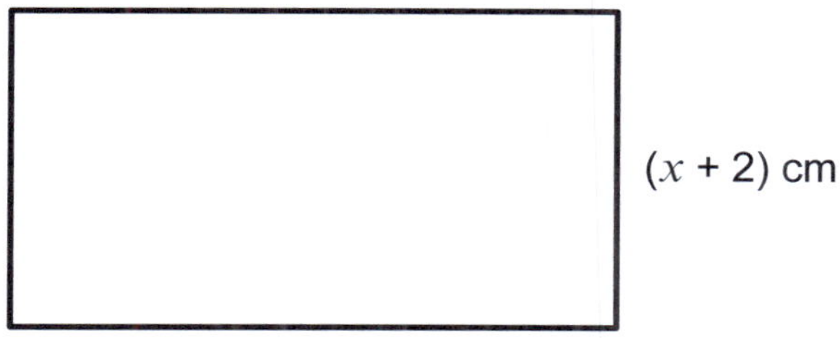


**a)** Write an expression for the perimeter of the rectangle. Give your answer in simplified form. **(3 marks)**

The perimeter of the rectangle is 72 cm.

**b)** Find the value of $x$. **(3 marks)**

**E5.** The table shows information about the weekly earnings of 20 people who work in a market.

| Weekly earnings, $x$ (£) | Frequency |
|---|---|
| $100 \leqslant x < 200$ | 2 |
| $200 \leqslant x < 300$ | 15 |
| $300 \leqslant x < 400$ | 2 |
| $400 \leqslant x < 500$ | 0 |
| $500 \leqslant x < 600$ | 1 |

**a)** Work out an estimate for the mean of the weekly earnings. **(4 marks)**

Rafa says, 'The mean may not be the best average to represent this information.'

**b)** Do you agree with Rafa? You must justify your answer. **(1 mark)**

**E6.** Courtney asks a group of children whether they like swimming or playing football.

Five children like both swimming and football.

14 children like swimming only.

18 children like playing football.

Three children do not like swimming or football.

How many children did Courtney ask?

**(3 marks)**

Use the Venn diagram to help you.

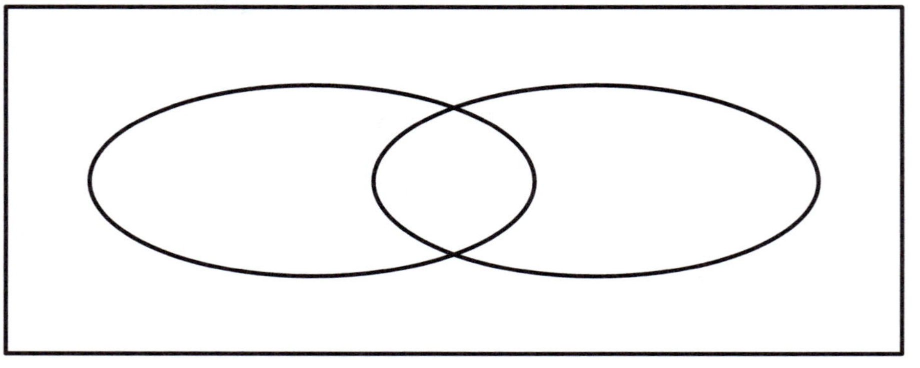

**E7.** Team A takes part in a quiz with 20 rounds.

After 8 rounds, team A has a mean score per round of 16.

For the next 12 rounds, team A has a mean score of 18.

What is the mean score per round for the whole quiz? **(4 marks)**

**E8.** Tiles are sold in packs of 30 tiles.

A pack of 30 tiles normally costs £24.80

Mary gets a discount of 25% off the cost of the packs.

Mary has £100

Work out the number of tiles Mary can buy. **(4 marks)**

**E9.** Jeremy invests £600 for 5 years in a savings account.

By the end of the 5 years he has received a total of £75 simple interest.

Work out the annual rate of simple interest. **(3 marks)**

**E10.** Amber is 6 years older than Jay.

Paul is twice as old as Amber.

The sum of the three ages is 54.

Find the ratio of Jay's age to Amber's age to Paul's age.

Give your answer as a ratio in its simplest form. **(5 marks)**

# End of Chapter Notes

It is good to keep a record of your learning when it is still fresh in your mind.

Copy this into your exercise book and complete it for each chapter.

Write 3 things you feel you have improved on.

| 1. |
|---|
| 2. |
| 3. |

Write 3 things you feel you need to keep an eye on.

| 1. |
|---|
| 2. |
| 3. |

Write 3 common mistakes that either you or your friends may make.

You could write specific mistakes or whole questions that you feel are easy to make a mistake on.

| 1. |
|---|
| 2. |
| 3. |

**Well done for completing this chapter and the whole book! You are AMAZING!**

# Foundation A
# Answers

## Chapter 1 – Algebra

### Set A

**A1.** $T = 6d + 15f$

**A2.** $T = 4n + 5$

**A3.** **a)** $20x$
**b)** $20x - 5$
**c)** 13 rows of seats

**A4.** **a)** $T = 5y + 9$
**b)** 9 cm

**A5.** **a)** $20 - t$
**b)** $4x + 20y$

**A6.** **a)** $1 - x$
**b)** $150 - 150x$

**A7.** **a)** area of rectangle A = area of rectangle B
$3(6x - 7) = 15x$
$18x - 21 = 15x$
**b)** $x = 7$
**c)** 52 cm

**A8.** **a)** 2
**b)** 6.5
**c)** $x = 8$

**A9.** **a)** £10
**b)** £45

**A10.** **a)** $4x + 2$
**b)** Mahalia: 17 books, Kirsten: 19 books, Ben: 34 books

### Set B

**B1.** **a)** $10 - 2x$
**b)** $10 + x$
**c)** 6 cherries

**B2.** **a)** $2x + 3$
**b)** 21 years

**B3.** **a)** total area $= 1(x + 2) + 3(x + 4)$
$= x + 2 + 3x + 12 = 4x + 14$
$= 2(2x + 7)$
**b)** 55 cm

**B4.** **a)** $12x + 18$ cm
**b)** $4x + 6$ cm

**B5.** **a)** $5x + 13$
**b)** 11A sold = 19, 11B sold = 38, 11C sold = 51

**B6.** **a)** length of each vertical side $= 3x$
length of each horizontal side $= 3x + y + y = 3x + 2y$
$P = 3x + 3x + (3x + 2y) + (3x + 2y) = 12x + 4y$
**b)** length of each horizontal side $= 3x$
length of each vertical side $= 3x - y - y = 3x - 2y$
$K = 3x + 3x + (3x - 2y) + (3x - 2y) = 12x - 4y$

**B7.** **a)** $(x + 5) + (x + 2a) + (a + 10) = 180°$
$2x + 3a + 15 = 180°$
$2x + 3a = 165°$
**b)** $y + (x + 5°) = 180°$
$y = 180° - (x + 5°)$
$y = 180° - x - 5°$
$y = 175° - x$

**B8.** **a)** line 3: she incorrectly adds $-x - 5x$; this should be $-6x$
line 7: she incorrectly divides $-1$ by 9; $x$ should equal $-\frac{1}{9}$
**b)** $x = -\frac{1}{11}$

**B9.** $x = 9$

**B10.** **a)** perimeter $= 2(3x - 2) + 2(2x - 3) + 2(2x + 6)$
$= 14x + 2$
perimeter = 86 cm so
$14x + 2 = 86$
**b)** $x = 6$ cm

### Set C

**C1.** **a)** $y - 4 + 13 = 2 \times y$
$y + 9 = 2y$
**b)** 9

**C2. a)** Elias has $x$, Arthur has $2 \times x = 2x$, Charlie has $2x + 9$

$x + 2x + 2x + 9 = 64$

$5x + 9 = 64$

**b)** 11 cards

**C3.** Box A: 27 oranges, Box B: 83 oranges, Box C: 50 oranges

**C4.** 17 years old

**C5. a)** perimeter $= x + 2x + (x + 1)$ $= 4x + 1$

perimeter = 38 cm so $4x + 1 = 38$

**b)** 18.5 cm

**C6.** 72 shells

**C7. a)** AD = $x$ cm, BC = $x + 1$ cm, AB = $2 \times x = 2x$ cm, DC = $(2x + 5)$ cm

perimeter $= x + (x + 1) + 2x + (2x + 5) = 6x + 6$

$6x + 6 = 78$

$3x + 3 = 39$

**b)** 12 cm

**C8.** 46 cm

**C9. a)** Holly's age $= x$, Leon's age $= 2 \times x = 2x$, Talya's age $= 2x - 3$

$x + 2x + (2x - 3) = 52$

$5x - 3 = 52$

**b)** 19 years old

**C10.** 34 students

## Set D

**D1.** 9 pens in each box

**D2.** £46

**D3. a)** $2x$

**b)** $0.75 - 3x$

**c)** $x = 0.18$

**D4. a)** area of trapezium ABCD

$= \frac{(7 + 2x + 7) \times 6}{2} = (14 + 2x) \times 3$

$(14 + 2x) \times 3 = 90$

$14 + 2x = 30$

**b)** 39 cm

**D5.** 112°

**D6. a)** If $x = 1$ cm then AB $= 4(1) - 6 = 4 - 6 = -2$

This can't be true as lengths must be positive.

**b)** $x = 7$ cm

**D7. a)** perimeter $= 4x + (x + 2) + (x + 2) + 3(x + 2) + 3(x + 2)$ $= 12x + 16$

$12x + 16 = 112$

$3x + 4 = 28$

**b)** 32 cm

**D8. a)** for example, let $x = 2$ and $y = 4$

$3 \times (2 + 4) = 3\ (6) = 18$

18 is a multiple of 6

**b)** for example, let $x = 3$, $y = 5$

$3 + 5 = 8$ and 8 is a multiple of 4 because $8 = 4 \times 2$

**D9.** area of ABCD $= (8 + x)(3 + x)$

$(8 + x)(3 + x) = 50$

$24 + 8x + 3x + x^2 = 50$

$24 + 11x + x^2 = 50$

$x^2 + 11x + 24 = 50$

$x^2 + 11x = 26$

**D10.** area of triangle ABF

$= \frac{1}{2} \times (x + 8) \times 8 = 4 \times (x + 8)$

$= (4x + 32)\ \text{cm}^2$

## Set E

**E1.** $d = 140°$

**E2. a)** 130

**b)** 70

**c)** 280

**d)** 260

**E3.** **a)** 25
**b)** 57
**c)** 51
**d)** 100

**E4.** $a = -1$

**E5.** gradient = $\frac{3x - 2}{4x - x} = \frac{x}{3x} = \frac{1}{3}$

**E6.** side length of square = 10 cm, area of square = 100 cm$^2$
area of circle = 25π cm$^2$
shaded area = area of square − area of circle
= 100 − 25π
= 25(4 − π) cm$^2$

**E7.** **a)** $x = 23°$
**b)** $y = 56°$

**E8.** **a)** $x = 40°$
**b)** $y = 40°$

**E9.** **a)** $x = 40°$
**b)** 160°

**E10.** **a)** $4x + 36$
**b)** Orlaigh: 50 marks, Maya: 62 marks, Arthur: 124 marks

## Chapter 2 – Ratio and proportion

### Set A

**A1.** 36°

**A2.** 12 matches

**A3.** Amy is correct.

**A4.** 80°

**A5.** 70°

**A6.** 1 : 2 : 3

**A7.** $n = 2.4$

**A8.** 1 : 6

**A9.** 10 fewer days

**A10.** **a)** 48 days
**b)** 12 days

### Set B

**B1.** 6 days

**B2.** **a)** **i)** 4 hours
**ii)** 1 hour
**b)** The rate of flow of water from each tap is the same.

**B3.** £211.20

**B4.** 9 shells

**B5.** **a)** 4 : 3
**b)** 3 : 4

**B6.** 40 cows

**B7.** 99 students

**B8.** 98 vans

**B9.** 144 orange highlighters

**B10.** 70 red pens

### Set C

**C1.** 8 red tiles

**C2.** $x = 2$ cm

**C3.** Sasha is not correct.

**C4.** 40 blue cubes

**C5.** 105 large boxes

**C6.** **a)** 22.5 m of wood, 15 wooden trays, 90 nails
**b)** 10.5 m of wood, 7 wooden trays, 42 nails

**C7.** **a)** 36 days
**b)** 3 days

**C8.** £56

**C9.** Four packs of butter

**C10.** butter = 180 g, brown sugar = 210 g, oats = 450 g, syrup = 3 tablespoons

### Set D

**D1.** 90 biscuits

**D2.** 32 biscuits

**D3.** 1400 ml lemonade

**D4.** **a)** 1 : 2 : 6

**b)** 1800 kg

**D5.** 1 : 2

**D6.** Daniel is correct.

**D7.** 44 stamps

**D8.** Helen saves the greatest percentage of her salary.

**D9.** 1 : 3

**D10.** 105 students

### Set E

**E1.** 76 balloons

**E2.** 8 jars

**E3.** 5 : 4 : 10

**E4.** 34%

**E5.** 16%

**E6.** 70%

**E7.** (12, 13)

**E8.** (3, 6)

**E9.** 90 cm

**E10.** 4.48 $m^2$

## Chapter 3 – Money

### Set A

**A1.** £243

**A2.** £6045

**A3.** Bank X

**A4.** **a)** Ben

**b)** No. The interest Ben receives will increase and Ben already receives more interest than Ali.

**A5.** 3%

**A6.** Bank Y

**A7.** £6.50

**A8.** **a)** 6 jars

**b)** No, Tahlia is not correct.

**A9.** £4

**A10.** 6 cards

### Set B

**B1.** £425

**B2.** Maisie is not correct.

**B3.** £8.00

**B4.** 20%

**B5.** 30%

**B6.** The village house has the greater value.

**B7.** Lucas does not have enough money to buy the laptop.

**B8.** Trainers are cheaper in the USA.

**B9.** Rehan does not have enough money.

**B10.** £4440

### Set C

**C1.** 25%

**C2.** Shop A has the better deal.

**C3.** The manager is not correct.

**C4.** **a)** £48

**b)** All the numbers were rounded down. The answer is an underestimate.

**C5.** **a)** £3.24

**b)** £0.38 or 38p

**C6.** **a)** £6.80

**b)** £1.36

**C7.** **a)** 5 hours 30 minutes

**b)** £34.10

**C8.** Aisha should get deal A as it is the cheapest.

**C9.** **a)** 21p

**b)** £63

**C10.** 49

### Set D

**D1.** £60

**D2.** £60

**D3.** Olly should get deal B as it is the cheapest.

**D4.** **a)** Option 1 is the cheapest.
**b)** Option 3 is the most expensive.

**D5.** £5.00

**D6.** 78% (2 s.f.)

**D7.** 3 : 5

**D8.** 4.75% (2 d.p.)

**D9.** **a)** Eva has rounded the numbers up.
**b)** £197.30

**D10.** £1564

### Set E

**E1.** 43

**E2.** £3937.50

**E3.** total pay = £190.40 < 200

**E4.** £300

**E5.** £118

**E6.** £9.50

**E7.** 15%

**E8.** £819

**E9.** 12.05 pm

**E10.** $x$ = £7.30/hour

## Chapter 4 – Data

### Set A

**A1.** 14 wear neither a watch nor glasses

**A2.** 4 neither sing or play an instrument

**A3.** $\frac{14}{29}$

**A4.** **a)** 4 boys do not have school lunch
**b)** $\frac{4}{15}$

**A5.** **a)** 7
**b)** 7
**c)** 4
**d)** Fleur is correct.

**A6.** 7, 7, 9, 10, 17

**A7.** 2, 3, 6, 7, 7

**A8.** **a)** 2
**b)** 1.8
**c)** 2
**d)** The team scored 3 goals in each of the 11th and 12th games.

**A9.** **a)** 27
**b)** £6
**c)** £2
**d)** £2 to the nearest pound

**A10.** **a)** The total distance is the not the total of the midpoint values. Instead, he should have multiplied the midpoint by the number of days and then found the total.

Stuart should have divided by the total number of days, which is 30, instead of dividing by 4.

**b)** 7.73 miles per day

### Set B

**B1.** 3 fish are golden and do not have stripes

**B2.** Valma asked 32 children

**B3.** 40 jars

**B4.** **a)** 43 cars
**b)** $\frac{59}{182}$

**B5.** 7 km

**B6.** **a)**

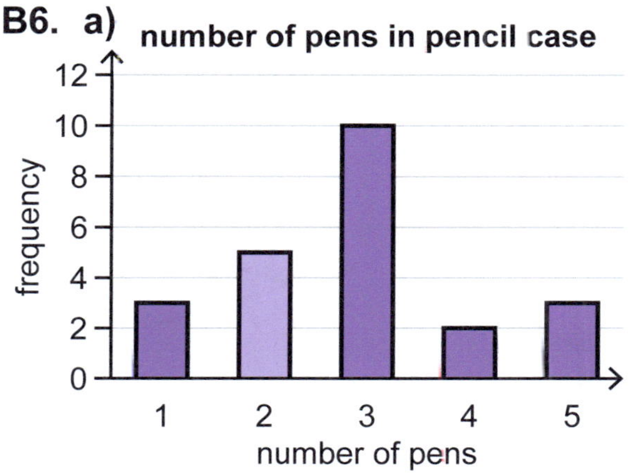


**b)** 23 children

**c)** 66 pens

**d)** $\frac{15}{23}$

**B7.** Tuesday and Thursday

**B8.** **a)** 50 boxes

**b)**

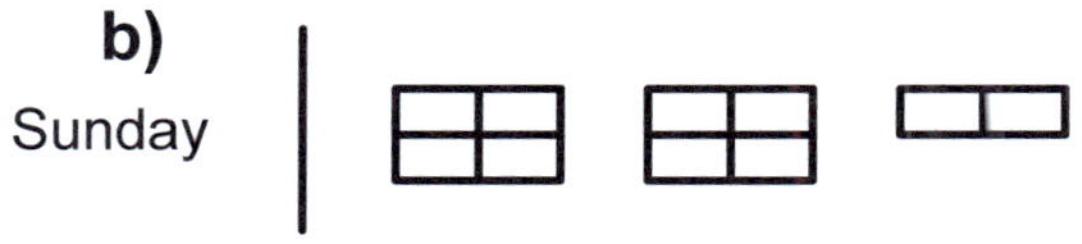


**B9.**

| Month | Number of customers | Angle in the pie chart |
|---|---|---|
| May | 10 | 40° |
| June | 35 | 140° |
| July | 30 | 120° |
| August | 15 | 60° |
| Total | 90 customers | 360° |

**B10.** $\frac{3}{8}$

## Set C

**C1.** 9 children play piano

**C2.** $\frac{3}{19}$

**C3.** **a)** $\frac{1}{8}$

**b)** 480

**c)** $\frac{7}{8}$

**C4.** 60 children

**C5.** **a)** **(i)** 24

**(ii)** 288

**b)** $\frac{1}{3}$

**C6.** **a)** 25%

**b)** $\frac{1}{6}$

**c)** 720 people

**C7.** **a)** 72 students

**b)** $\frac{7}{36}$

**C8.** **a)** 0.15

**b)** 12 red counters

**C9.** **a)**

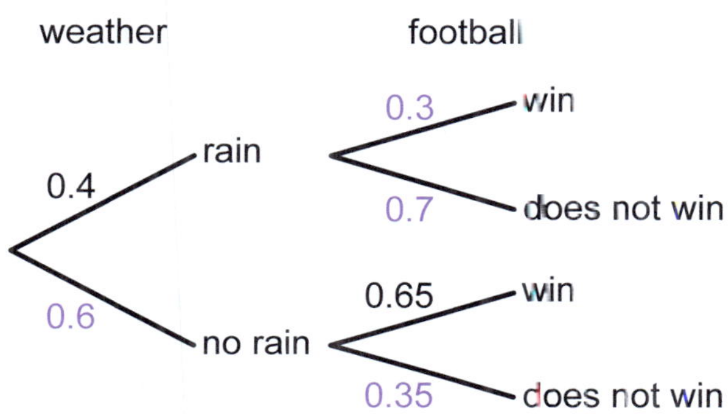


**b)** 0.51

**C10.** **a)**

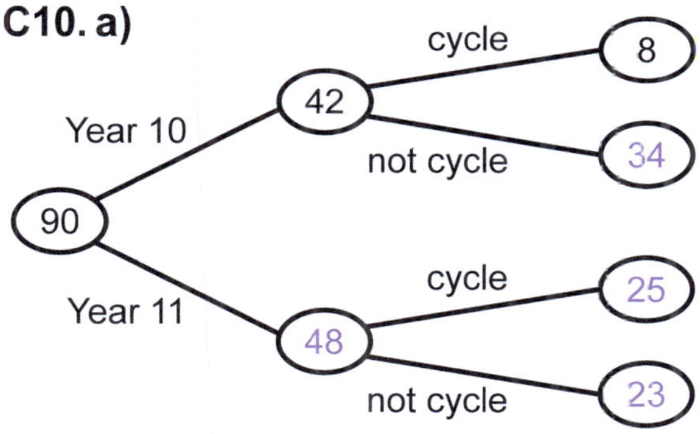


**b)** $\frac{23}{48}$

## Set D

**D1.** 23 people own either a cat or a dog, but not both

**D2.** **a)** 26 students

**b)** $\frac{7}{13}$

**D3.** **a)** P(3) = 0.15

**b)** 24 times

**D4.** **a)** 20 matches

**b)** 45 goals

**c)** 2.25

**D5.** 3 minutes and 10 seconds

**D6.** 162.4 cm

**D7.** **a)** 8 days

**b)** 1.7 minutes

**c)** 1 minute

**d)** 6 minutes

**e)** 0 minutes

**D8.** The $x$-axis is should be labelled.

There should be a 0 at the bottom of the vertical axis.

The height of the fourth column is incorrect. It should be 5.

**D9.** The line of best fit is not drawn correctly. It should be drawn so that there are approximately equal number of points above and below it, and it should be as close as possible to all the data points.

The numbers on the $x$-axis go from 145 to 155; 150 is missing.

It should be 145, 150, 155

The numbers on the $y$-axis should start from 45, not 40 as the numbers increase in 5s.

**D10.** The $x$-axis should be labelled 'Mass (g)'.

The first and last points should not be connected.

The point (15, 8) has been plotted incorrectly.

It should have been plotted at (17.5, 8).

## Set E

**E1.** 7, 7, 4, so range is 3

**E2.** **a)**

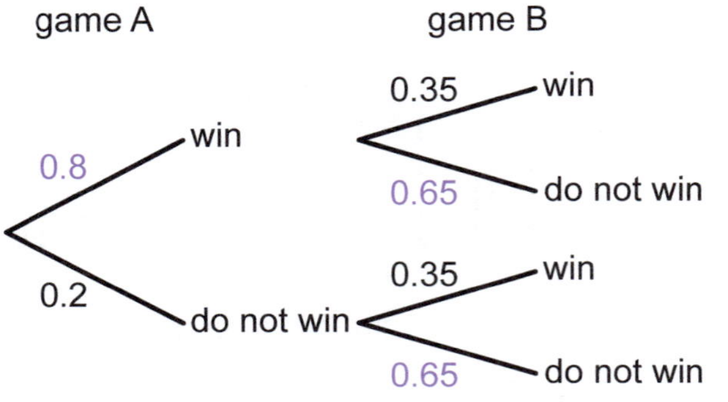


**b)** 0.28

**E3.** Incorrect key; units should be years.

Missing entry – there should be two at 28.

Incorrect order in the 3 leaf: 34 should come before 35.

**E4.** **a)** 164 cm

**b)** Archie is not correct.

**E5.** **a)**

| Number of minutes, $M$ | Frequency |
|---|---|
| $0 \leqslant M < 30$ | 5 |
| $30 \leqslant M < 60$ | 6 |
| $60 \leqslant M < 90$ | 8 |
| $90 \leqslant M < 120$ | 9 |
| $120 \leqslant M < 150$ | 2 |

**b)** 1.2 hours per day

**c)** $\frac{11}{30}$

**E6.** $\frac{2}{21}$

**E7. a)**

| | Rome | Milan | Total |
|---|---|---|---|
| **Business class** | 41 | 29 | 70 |
| **Economy class** | 41 | 89 | 130 |
| **Total** | 82 | 118 | 200 |

**b)** $\frac{41}{200}$

**E8.** Median = 2

**E9.** 251 km

**E10. a)**

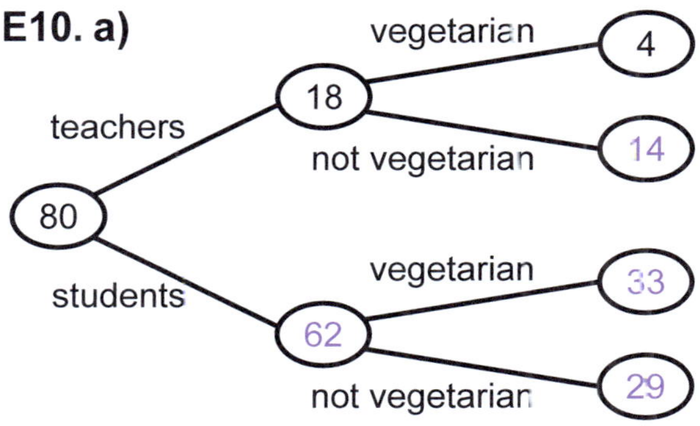


**b)** $\frac{29}{62}$

## Chapter 5 – Mixed questions

### Set A

**A1. a)** $T = 2x + 3p$

**b)** $x = 182$ cm

**A2. a)**

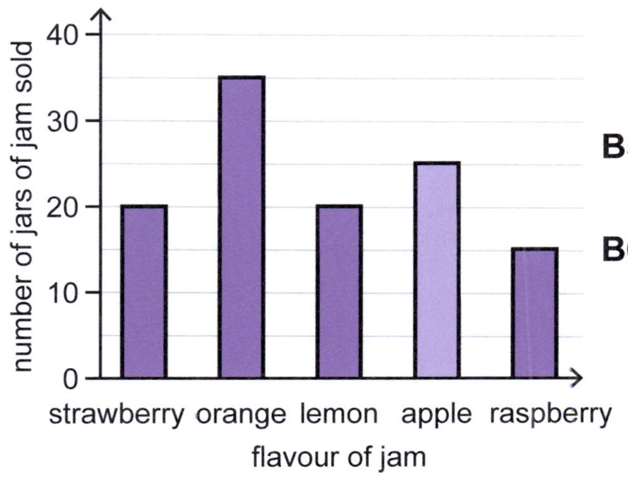


**b)** 7 : 3

**c)** Xavi is incorrect.

**A3.** 80

**A4.** £36.20

**A5. a)** 24 minutes

**b)** The water from each tap flows at the same rate.

**A6.** 2 tins

**A7. a)** 7 students play tennis only

**b)** $\frac{5}{14}$

**A8.** £36

**A9.** 60 biscuits

**A10. a)** perimeter $= 2(x + 7) + 2(x - 4) = 126$

$2x + 14 + 2x - 8 = 126$

$4x + 6 = 126$

$2x + 3 = 63$

**b)** 962 cm$^2$

### Set B

**B1.** £544

**B2.** £114.40

**B3. a)** 5 penalties

**b)** 3 penalties

**c)** 2.275… = 2 penalties (nearest whole number)

**B4. a)** 6 boxes

**b)** No, Matilda is incorrect. She can buy 13 boxes instead of 12.

**B5. a)** 115

**b)** 16

**B6. a)** 12.5 m

**b)** Range in Verulanium Park < Range in Abbotts Hill Park, since 4.1 < 5.9

This suggests that the heights of the trees in Abbotts Hill are more spread.

Median in Verulanium Park > Median in Abbotts Hill Park, since 12.5 > 10.1

This suggests that, on average, Verulanium Park's trees are taller than the ones in Abbotts Hill.

**B7.** £162

**B8.** 24 m

**B9.** **a)**

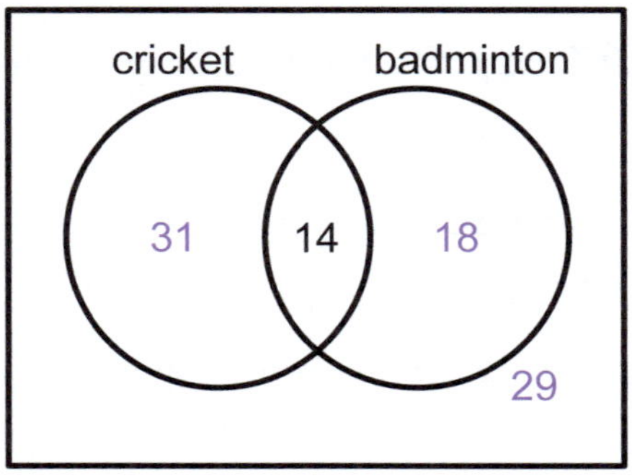


**b)** $\frac{29}{92}$

**B10.** £65

## Set C

**C1.** **a)** multiplier = 100% + 4% = 104% = 1.04 not 1.4

She has used an incorrect multiplier.

**b)** multiplier = 100% − 3% = 97% = 0.97

He has used an incorrect multiplier.

**C2.** **a)** 10 cakes

**b)** Friday 

**c)** £1242

**C3.** 6

**C4.** 44°

**C5.** £102

**C6.** Personal Bank gives more interest.

**C7.** **a)** 11 miles

**b)** 6 miles

**c)** $x = 10$

**C8.** 99 cm

**C9.** $T = 10s + 12l$

**C10.** **a)**

| | Milk chocolate | Dark chocolate | Total |
|---|---|---|---|
| **Star shape** | 2 | 8 | 10 |
| **Rectangular shape** | 18 | 4 | 22 |
| **Total** | 20 | 12 | 32 |

**b)** 9 : 2

## Set D

**D1.** **a)** £8.75

**b)** £5.25

**D2.** $x = 2.5\%$

**D3.** **a)** 5

**b)** 2.5 (1 d.p.)

**D4.** **a)** $x = 0.5$

**b)** 6 cm$^2$

**D5.** £5451.78

**D6.** **a)** $x = 6$ days, $y = 8$ days

**b)** 6.0 cm/day (1 decimal place)

**D7.** £12 272.71

**D8.** **a)**

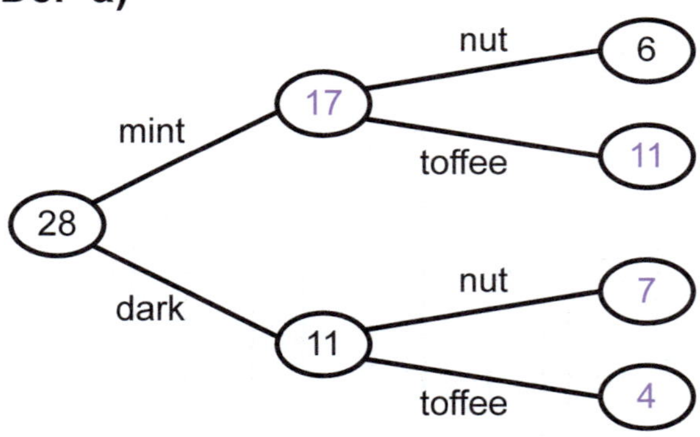


**b)** $\frac{1}{4}$

**D9.** **a)** $x = 3$ cm

**b)** 24 cm$^2$

**D10. a)**

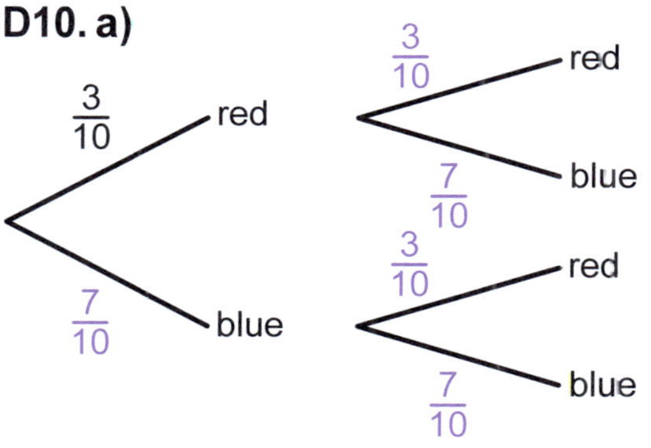


**b)** $\frac{29}{50}$

## Set E

**E1.** £15

**E2.** £3 more

**E3.** 5 labradors not on a lead

**E4. a)** perimeter = $6x + 12$

**b)** $x = 10$ cm

**E5. a)** £265

**b)** Use Median or mode instead of mean as they are not affected by extreme values like the one person in the $55 < x < 600$ class.
Rafa is correct. (1 mark)

Accept

Rafa is not correct.

**E6.** 35 children

**E7.** 17.2 points

**E8.** 150 tiles

**E9.** 2.5%

**E10.** 3 : 5 : 10

# Index